An Approach to PATERSON

NEW HAVEN AND LONDON, YALE UNIVERSITY PRESS

1967

An Approach to

PATERSON

by *Walter Scott Peterson*

Library of Congress catalog card number: 67–24510

Grateful acknowledgment is extended to New
Directions Publishing Corporation for permission
to quote from the following works by
William Carlos Williams:
Paterson, copyright 1946, 1949, 1951, © 1958
by William Carlos Williams, copyright © 1963
by Florence Williams
*The Collected Earlier Poems of William Carlos
Williams,* copyright 1938, 1951 by William
Carlos Williams
*The Collected Later Poems of William Carlos
Williams,* copyright 1944, 1948, 1950 by
William Carlos Williams
Pictures from Brueghel and Other Poems, copyright
1954, 1955, © 1959 by William Carlos Williams
In the American Grain, copyright 1925 by James
Laughlin, 1933 by William Carlos Williams

Yale College Series

The tradition of undergraduate writing and publishing has long been a very lively one at Yale, as witnessed by the large number of periodicals, journalistic or literary in character, which have appeared on the Yale campus. These, however, fail to give an accurate picture of the high proportion of good and original scholarly writing which is also done by undergraduates. The excellence of many of the Honors theses written by Yale Seniors made it desirable some years ago to give the most deserving of them the circulation which publication in printed form could provide. Between 1941 and 1957 ten volumes were published in the Undergraduate Prize Essays Series and two in the Scholars of the House Series. The authors of several of these essays have gone on to fulfill amply the promise of their early scholarly efforts. More recently the growing number of theses of outstanding merit has encouraged Yale College and the Yale University Press to establish this new YALE COLLEGE SERIES with the hope that every year it will be possible to publish some of the best work by the Honors majors in the Senior Class. The selection, which is necessarily a very rigorous one, was performed for the Class of 1966 by a faculty committee made up of Messrs. M. I. J. Griffin, David Calleo, and E. M. Waith, Chairman.

Georges May
Dean of Yale College

FOR MY PARENTS

Introduction:
A Plan for Action
to Supplant a Plan for Action

William Carlos Williams' *Paterson* is a poem which celebrates the power of human love and imagination. As Williams puts it in *Asphodel, That Greeny Flower,* a poem he composed in the decade before his death:

> Light, the imagination
> > and love,
> > > in our age,
> by natural law,
> > which we worship,
> > > maintain
> all of a piece
> > their dominance.   [*PB* 180]

Williams' critics sometimes characterize *Paterson* as a poem about the failure of love and imagination, but it does not seem to me that such a characterization can be altogether correct. Breakdown and failure are important in the poem, but this does not exclude the possibility of fulfillment. *Paterson* involves a positive as well as a negative attitude toward life, a positive as well as a negative way of viewing and responding to the given "realities" of existence.

Aside from *Paterson,* Williams' most important discussion of these conflicting attitudes occurs in *In the American Grain* (1925), a collection of what might well be called imaginative historical essays.

I

The title refers not so much to a single attitude as to two attitudes, both of which are firmly "ingrained" in the complex texture of American culture. Broadly speaking, *In the American Grain* is a symbolic formulation of an American historio-aesthetic myth. That is to say, it sets forth a vision of the past, present, and future not only of American man but also of American art. Since the section entitled "Père Sebastian Rasles," which occurs almost exactly at the book's center, is the most inclusive statement of this myth, it is this section with which I shall be mainly concerned here,[1] although I shall also suggest the thematic relevance of most of the work's remaining parts.

The essay is concerned with two opposing states of mind, one associated with the Puritans, especially Cotton Mather, and the other associated with the French Catholic missionaries to the Indians, especially Père Sebastian Rasles. The "Puritan" is developed first, and Williams begins his argument by introducing his "rigid tenet" that the Puritans were "seeds of Elizabethan vigor" (110) that ultimately failed to take root and mature. In an earlier section called "Voyage of the Mayflower" we read: "In those little pips a nadir, sure as the sun, was reached, in which lay the character of beginnings in North America. As particles stripped of wealth, mortifying as they were mortified, *"predicateurs,"* greatly suffering, greatly prepared to suffer, they were the perfect sprout for the savage continent God had driven them to" (63). The Puritans endured, then, to found the American nation, but the means by which they endured—the seed's protective shell, to continue Williams' metaphor (112)—derived from fear, isolation, and negation: "If they were pure it was more since they had nothing in them of fulfillment than because of positive virtues" (63). Isolated and narrowly turned in on themselves, they failed in three of the most important ways by which man achieves the truly Human. Regarding the New World itself, "the greatest wonder of the world" (26), they only "closed it out" (112). Regarding each other, especially in the sexual sense, they were equally solipsistic: Puritanism's "virtue"

1. My discussion owes much to the important essay by Louis L. Martz, "The Unicorn in *Paterson:* William Carlos Williams," *Thought,* 35 (1960), 537–54.

Preface

All quotations from *Paterson* are from the complete edition published in 1963 by New Directions. Since the organization of this study follows the organization of the poem itself, I have identified the source of quoted passages only when they are quoted out of their normal context. According to the system I have used, the citation 130:7–131:20 is a reference to page 130, line 7, through page 131, line 20—where every printed line of poetry or prose is counted (they are not numbered in the text). The same system applies to the cross references.

In its original form this study was presented as a senior honors essay to the Yale College Faculty of English. It is the direct result of the stimulation I received in an undergraduate seminar on modern poetry conducted by Louis L. Martz and Harold Bloom. My profound indebtedness to both should be apparent throughout the pages which follow. To Professor Martz, my adviser, I owe a special debt of gratitude for his many suggestions, always enlightening, yet never dogmatic. Invaluable assistance and encouragement have also been given by Clifford Earl Ramsey and Ajodhia N. Kaul, who read and criticized portions of the manuscript, by Michael J. K. O'Loughlin and Davis P. Harding, who are in charge of the intensive major in English, and by Wayland Schmitt, my editor. In addition, I wish to thank all others who, often unbeknownst to me, have read my manuscript and forwarded it in its course toward publication, especially the committees for the Wrexham and Lloyd Mifflin Prizes. I must also thank those friends, particularly Robert M. Rosa and Robert L. Reid, who have helped me with their comments and criticisms, and all those who have suffered a young author's enthusiasm and preoccupation. Finally, for their continuous encouragement and support, I render public thanks to my parents: my gratitude to them the dedication can only begin to express.

W.S.P.

New Haven, Connecticut
January 2, 1967

Contents

Preface   **ix**

Abbreviations   **xiii**

*Introduction: A Plan for Action to Supplant
A Plan for Action*   **1**

1. *The Delineaments of the Giants:* PATERSON, BOOK ONE   **18**

2. *Sunday in the Park:* PATERSON, BOOK TWO   **44**
      A World Which I Approach Concretely   **44**
      The Voice of the Evangelist   **78**
      The Descent Beckons   **100**

3. *The Library:* PATERSON, BOOK THREE   **118**
      A Song to Make Death Tolerable   **118**
      Touched by the Fire   **142**
      Beside the Sliding Water   **161**

4. *The Run to the Sea:* PATERSON, BOOK FOUR   **184**

   Index   **215**

Abbreviations

CEP   *The Collected Earlier Poems of William Carlos Williams,* Norfolk, Conn., New Directions, 1951.

CLP   *The Collected Later Poems of William Carlos Williams,* rev. ed. Norfolk, Conn., New Directions, 1963.

Grain   *In the American Grain,* Norfolk, Conn., New Directions, 1956.

P   *Paterson,* Norfolk, Conn., New Directions, 1963.

PB   *Pictures from Brueghel and Other Poems,* Norfolk, Conn., New Directions, 1962.

If a man die
                it is because death
                              has first
possessed his imagination. . . .
But love and the imagination
                are of a piece,
                              swift as the light
to avoid destruction.

    Asphodel, That Greeny Flower

      today
      the particulars
      of poetry

      that difficult art
      require
      your whole attention.

        The Thoughtful Lover

I wanted to write a poem
that you would understand
For what good is it to me
if you can't understand it?
                But you got to try hard.

    January Morning

was "to make each man stand alone ... A husband, after twenty years, [knew] his wife's body not more than neck and ankles" (111–12). They "could not afford to allow their senses to wander any more than they could allow a member of their company to wander from the precinct of the church, even from Boston to Casco Bay" (111). Finally, even their minds were confined, and imaginative exploration was as rigidly proscribed as was geographic and sensual exploration: "Each shrank from an imagination that would sever him from the rest" (65). In consequence of these failures, according to Williams' definitions, the Puritans were both "inhuman" and "immoral," and the inhumanity and immorality they founded is present in American culture today.

Williams conceives Père Rasles as the direct antithesis of the Puritans. Most important was Rasles' generous attitude toward the Indians, who themselves embodied a great deal that Williams sees as truly "American." Like Daniel Boone, about whom Williams writes in a later essay, Rasles "saw the truth of the Red Man, not an aberrant type, treacherous and anti-white to be feared and exterminated, but as a natural expression of the place, the Indian himself as 'right,' the flower of his world" (137). The Puritans "never realized the Indian in the least save as an unformed PURITAN" (113); and even then they exploited the Indians, gradually took over Indian lands, and when the Indians finally retaliated, pursued "a relentless lust for [their] extermination" (117). The Puritans, in short, never "touched" the Indians. Father Rasles, on the contrary, not only "touched" the natives "every day" (120), but admired them (122, 126), lived among them, learned their language (121), and finally almost became one of them (123, 126). Rasles was also responsive to the "wonder" of the land (120). In his relationship with both the New World's inhabitants and the New World itself, he was "a spirit, rich, blossoming, generous, able to give and to receive, full of taste, a nose, a tongue" (120). As this quotation suggests, even Rasles' senses were not wholly to be denied, although since Rasles was a priest, Williams requires other symbolic personages to develop this aspect of his aesthetic to its fullest. Jacataqua, for example, in the section bearing

3

her name as its title, is described as "yielding to the wild pulses of her heart" (187). And Aaron Burr, in the section entitled "The Virtue of History," is described as one in whom "there burned a spring-time of the soul, a mounting desire that makes him seem, beside the harness animals of that dawning period like a bird in flight" (196). In any event, while the Puritans were nothing but "blind seeds," Rasles "blossomed" and "lived." He replaced solipsism with mutuality and generosity, and exclusiveness with a pervasive inclusiveness.

"Yet in secret," the Puritans "tried without ceasing to kill the offending Jesuit. He *was* killed by them at last . . . and they mangled him besides" (127). This completes the historic side of Williams' myth to the present, and although both influences formed "the aesthetic and the moral fiber" (127) of America, the "Puritan" in-fluence is dominant as its opposite is submerged. The remainder of the myth is therefore the implied reemergence of that which is sym-bolized by Rasles: "All that will be new in America will be anti-Puritan. It will be of another root. It will be more from the heart of Rasles, in the north" (120). Such a prophecy is particularly im-portant when applied to aesthetics. What may be called the Rasles aesthetic has been much suppressed and to some extent even "killed," and a wholly Puritan aesthetic has in general supplanted it. But art's past is less interesting than art's future, and it is with the prophecy of new aesthetic beginnings that most of *In the American Grain* is really concerned.

The most important aspect of Williams' program for artistic re-newal is a "return to the ground." Perhaps the clearest statement of this occurs in the section called "Descent," concerning Sam Houston: "But he who will grow . . . must sink first. . . . He [must] have the feet of his understanding on the ground, his ground, *the* ground, the only ground that he knows, that which *is* under his feet. I speak of aesthetic satisfaction. This want, in America, can only be filled by knowledge, a poetic knowledge, of that ground" (213). "Knowledge of the ground," as a symbolic state, involves a number of different things. On one level it means simply a return to the land itself. To "know" America today, however, is not only to know the America which spread before Rasles (our humane and human source), although this is certainly a part of it, but also to be reconciled with the land as it is today—with the immediate particulars of the here and now. Thus Williams' well-known tenet, "no ideas but in things" (*P* 14:17), and his enormous concern for the "local." Williams does not, of course, avoid generalized philosophical ideas, but he does insist "on communication through tangible objects which may be more 'real' to the reader than abstract words."[2] In contrast to T. S. Eliot, who asserts in *Four Quartets* that "Place is only place," Williams' whole aesthetic is based on the belief that

> Place is the only reality, the true core of the universal. . . . We live only in one place at a time but far from being bound by it, only through it do we realize our freedom. Place then ceases to be a restriction, we do not have to abandon our familiar and known to achieve distinction but far from constricting ourselves, not searching for some release in some particular place, rather in that place, if we only make ourselves sufficiently aware of it, do join with others in other places.[3]

The "local" is not, to be sure, necessarily American—except *to* the American—and it can be any locality, so long as it *is* local to the poet: "America to me means any place, anywhere and just HAPPENS to mean America to me for the simple reason that it is . . . America."[4] Indeed, the local can even be an imaginative realm within the mind, as is the *"new locality"* associated with Poe (216). Williams does not, however, see the local as an end in itself, for the poet's goal is "to be both local (all art is local) and at the same time to surmount that

2. Linda Welshimer Wagner, *The Poems of William Carlos Williams: A Critical Study* (Middletown, Conn., Wesleyan University Press, 1963), p. 4.

3. "The Fatal Blunder," *Quarterly Review of Literature,* 2 (1944), 126.

4. Unpublished letter to James Laughlin, Jan. 20, 1939, William Carlos Williams Papers, Yale Collection of American Literature, Yale University Library, New Haven, Conn.

restriction by climbing to the universal in all art."[5] The local ultimately embodies the universal—indeed, is the universal—and this
is why

> so much depends
> upon
>
> a red wheel
> barrow
>
> glazed with rain
> water
>
> beside the white
> chickens.   [*CEP* 277]

The poet's relationship with his world must be inclusive, like
Rasles': "For everything his fine sense, blossoming, thriving, opening,
reviving—not shutting out—was tuned" (121). Such an impulse is
fundamental, "grounded" in still another sense of this important
word. It must be emphasized, however, that the "descent" is hazard-
ous, and that it can lead to an ultimate dissolution of self. In the
section called "De Soto and the New World," for example, a feminine
principle representing the land continually calls to De Soto, "you
are mine" (45), but the siren-like lyricism of her call is deceptive,
and ultimately leads the explorer to his death: "Down, down this
solitary sperm, down into the liquid, the formless, the insatiable belly
of sleep; down among the fishes: there was one called bagre, the third
part of which was head, with gills from end to end, and along the sides
were great spines, like very sharp awls" (58).[6] In comparison with

5. Letter to Henry Well, Apr. 12, 1950, *The Selected Letters of William
Carlos Williams,* ed. John C. Thirlwall (New York, McDowell, Obolensky,
1957), p. 286.
6. Cf. *P* 155:10–19.

Daniel Boone's and Sam Houston's successful "descents," De Soto's "failure" may be related to his greater passivity. His failure, in fact, seems similar to what D. H. Lawrence sees as Whitman's failure—namely, too great an absorption into formlessness.[7] Like Sam Patch, the famous diver in *Paterson* I, who, after a number of successful dives, finally fails to "come up" again, De Soto fails to make the descent a prelude to rebirth. It is against just such a failure that Williams warns Paterson near the end of *Paterson* IV.

This symbolic pattern—the contrast between the Puritans and Father Rasles—is developed throughout *In the American Grain* as a whole. The various sections, in fact, tend to alternate between these two poles in more or less regular fashion. The essay on Columbus, "The Discovery of the Indies," for example, is followed by an essay on Cortez, "The Destruction of Tenochtitlan." At the conclusion of the former section Columbus' sense of wonder in the presence of "the most beautiful thing which [he] had ever seen" (26)[8] is triumphantly affirmed, but in the section on Cortez and Montezuma, although Cortez is described as having been capable of aesthetic contemplation, we watch this virtue gradually becoming perverted by the desire to appropriate. Similarly, against "Voyage of the Mayflower," in which Williams describes the founding of our "Puritan" nation, he juxtaposes "The Founding of Quebec." In this latter essay he enthusiastically endorses Champlain as "a man after my own heart . . . the perfection of what we lack" (69). In the chapter called "The May-Pole at Merry Mount," while Thomas Morton's "vulgar royalist libertinism" (75) is condemned by the "Puritan Elders" and their various historians, Morton's energy and vitality, as manifested in the May Games, are clearly at one with the sentiments of the section's narrator. The perhaps overly lengthy extracts from the Salem witchcraft trials which make up most of the next section, "Cotton Mather's Wonders of the Invisible World," further develop the Puritan's in-

7. "Whitman," in his *Studies in Classic American Literature* (New York, Viking Press, 1964), pp. 163–77.

8. Cf. *P* 209: 9–14 and the references to the "Beautiful thing" in Book III.

sane "Trustless[ness] of humane experience," a trait introduced in the section on Morton (80). As the title suggests, the "Puritan" notion of "wonder" is diametrically opposed to Rasles', not only because it is perverse (Mather relates "a few of those Matchless Curiosities, with which the *Witchcraft* now upon us, has entertained us"—100), but also because it ignores the local given in favor of the "invisible."

In the second half of *In the American Grain,* after the chapter on Rasles, Williams continues to develop his central symbols. "The Discovery of Kentucky," which to some extent parallels "The Discovery of the Indies," is concerned with the story of Daniel Boone:

> There was, thank God, a great voluptuary born to the American settlements against the niggardliness of the damming puritanical tradition . . . Filled with the wild beauty of the New World to overbrimming so long as he had what he desired, to bathe in, to explore always more deeply, to see, to feel, to touch —his instincts were contented. Sensing a limitless fortune which daring could make his own, he sought only with primal lust to grow close to it, to understand it and to be part of its mysterious movements—like an Indian. And among all the colonists, like an Indian, the ecstasy of complete possession of the new country was his alone. In Kentucky he would stand, a lineal descendant of Columbus.   [130, 136–37]

The "forbidden wealth of the Unknown [West]" (131) which Boone sought was the frontier feared by the original Puritans, at a later stage in history. But Boone's "Natural choice" was toward the "new and unexplored country, invested with every beauty, every danger, every incident that could amuse the imagination or quicken action" (132). He turned his back to Europe, and sought for meaning in the interior "ground" of his native land.

Against this section, after a brief note on George Washington ("in a great many ways thoroughly disappointing"—143), Williams juxtaposes a discussion of Benjamin Franklin. The title, "Poor Richard," is intensely ironic, and the poverty involved here is essentially the poverty of which Wallace Stevens writes in the concluding section of *Esthétique du Mal:*

> The greatest poverty is not to live
> In a physical world, to feel that one's desire
> Is too difficult to tell from despair. . . .
> . . . . . The adventurer
> In humanity has not conceived of a race
> Completely physical in a physical world.

To a Boone, a Columbus, or a Rasles the world is enough if only man will accept it, but to a man like Franklin the "truth is, that though there are in [America] few people so miserable as the poor of Europe, there are also very few that in Europe would be called rich; it is rather a general happy mediocrity that prevails" (145). Even more important, the riches Franklin did see in the New World, he saw only as potentially "useful"—ripe for pragmatic exploitation and appropriation. He could not "quite leave hands off it [the New World] but must TOUCH it, in a 'practical' way, that is a joking, shy, nasty way, using 'science' etc., not with the generosity of the savage or scientist but in a shameful manner" (157). The final charge against Franklin is that he mechanically restrained what might otherwise have been vital and exuberant: "Franklin, along with all the responsible aristocrats of his period, shows the two major characteristics of a bulky, crude energy, something in proportion to the continent, and a colossal restraint equalizing it. The result must have been a complete cancellation, frustration or descent to a low plane for release, which latter alternative he chose shiningly" (153). This, basically, is the charge leveled against Franklin by D. H. Lawrence as well.[9]

Jacataqua and Aaron Burr, however, were virtually the apotheosis of energy. Both figures were "primitive and direct" (187). Their voluptuousness is much akin to Boone's (130), but more revolution-

9. "Benjamin Franklin," *Studies in Classic American Literature,* pp. 9–21.

ary and more specifically sexual. Especially in the section on Burr, parallels in Blake (to whom "Exuberance is Beauty") and D. H. Lawrence are unmistakable. Burr believed that "there is nothing on earth divine beside humanity" (188); he "refused to abide loyally by the established order" (196); he "saw America in his imagination, free" (197). Puritanism is Urizenic and constraining; life and art must, through imagination, break such bonds and acknowledge circumference only at the limits of desire:

> The world is made to eat, not leave, that the spirit may be full, not empty. [205]

> Those who restrain desire, do so because theirs is weak enough to be restrained; and the restrainer or reason usurps its place and governs the unwilling. [*The Marriage of Heaven and Hell*]

By now the basic qualities that Williams associates with each of his two opposing states of mind should be clear. The "Puritans," most simply, symbolize the kind of mind which, pursuing only pragmatic ends, views the world with mistrust or even fear. Such a mind seeks to isolate itself by retreating into conventionality and solipsism. Rasles and Williams' other heroes, on the contrary, symbolize the kind of mind which, pursuing only the wonder and beauty freely given by its local surroundings, views the world with trust and courage. Through love and imagination such a mind seeks a mutual relationship with its world that is both vital and creative. In the following pages I hope to show the relevance of these symbolic patterns to *Paterson*. In his epic, of course, Williams seldom refers to the symbols utilized in *In the American Grain;* he uses instead the equivalent terms "divorce" and "marriage." But however he may describe them, the two contrasting states of mind defined in *In the American Grain* loom behind both *Paterson* as a whole and the individual details of which it is composed. And the poem's argument, an argument summarized in the passage I have selected as my first epigraph, is that man's loving and imaginative "marriage" to the particulars of his local world can ultimately save him from the death-in-life of "Puritan divorce."

Such an elucidation of what I consider to be the meaning of the poem, however, is only a part of my aim in this study. As my second and third epigraphs suggest, Williams is a poet to whom details— the minute particulars making up the total fabric of the poem—are of the greatest importance. Unfortunately, none of the existing criticism on *Paterson* sets out to investigate, systematically and at length, just how these details work. That such an investigation is justified by the quality of Williams' material itself appears to me beyond question, and, to apply to the whole poem a statement made by Randall Jarrell when he reviewed *Paterson* I: "It seems a shame to write a little review of it, instead of going over it page by page, explaining and admiring. . . . There are hundreds of things in the poem that deserve specific mention."[10] This is not to say, however, that close analysis of every part of a tightly constructed poem of nearly three hundred pages is necessary or even desirable. Consequently, although I have included brief discussions of *Paterson* I (especially the introductory portion) and *Paterson* IV, I have focused mainly on *Paterson* II and III. These were originally the poem's central books, and they seem to me to be the most rewarding books of the poem. As for *Paterson* V, which was not added until some seven years after the original projected sequence was completed, although it enters my discussion at several points, I do not consider it at length because in many ways it seems more a poem about, or a product of, the earlier books than an integral part of the epic itself.[11] That is to say, Book V seems at most a kind of coda to the poem, for Books I through IV make up a complete and unified entity in themselves.

Paterson opens, tellingly, with a statement of themes that is characteristic of traditional epic. This statement is not specifically a part

10. "The Poet and his Public," *Partisan Review, 18* (1946), 493, 498.
11. See an excellent discussion of *Paterson* V by Martz, "The Unicorn in *Paterson*," pp. 537–54.

of Book I, but like the three-page "Preface" that follows it, it is ultimately an introduction to Williams' poem as a whole:

> : *a local pride; spring, summer, fall and the sea; a confession; a basket; a column; a reply to Greek and Latin with the bare hands; a gathering up; a celebration;*
>
> *in distinctive terms; by multiplication a reduction to one; daring; a fall; the clouds resolved into a sandy sluice; an enforced pause;*
>
> *hard put to it; an identification and a plan for action to supplant a plan for action; a taking up of slack; a dispersal and a metamorphosis.*

"A local pride," of course, underlies Williams' whole aesthetic. As I have said, he sees the local as the only source of the universal and insists unceasingly that "ideas" can be found only "in distinctive terms." Even more important, it is only particular things that the man of love and imagination can "marry." *Paterson,* then, is "a celebration," Williams' greatest celebration, of the "local." It is "a confession" of faith which is both a personal testament and a universal hymn.

Paterson's form, or lack of it, has often seemed an even greater problem to critics than its content. John Malcolm Brinnin, for example, has called it a " 'model of confusion' . . . a polyhedral view of experience, forcing the reader to witness as a fact the historical and spiritual dislocation that not only provides the poem with its theme but suggests its shape."[12] Similarly, Roy Harvey Pearce has written that "Williams *intends* that we see no clear structure in *Paterson.* . . . He admits that he is stuck with the things of his world as they are, and he will take them as they are."[13] Mimetic theories such as these are

12. *William Carlos Williams,* University of Minnesota Pamphlets on American Writers, No. 24 (Minneapolis, University of Minnesota Press, 1961), p. 115.

13. *The Continuity of American Poetry* (Princeton, Princeton University Press, 1961), p. 115.

certainly correct, as far as they go, and Williams intimates his aware-ness of them by calling his poem "a basket."[14] Yet the problems of such a conception of poetry are obvious. As Randall Jarrell, who described *Paterson's* structure as "Organization of Irrelevance," has put it: "Such organization is *ex post facto* organization: if something is somewhere, one can always find Some Good Reason for its being there, but if it had not been there would one reader have missed it? if it had been put somewhere else, would one reader have guessed where it should have 'really' gone?"[15] Still, Williams insists that his poem is "a column"—that is, something organized (like a column of men), something carefully made (like an architectural column), some-thing both "grounded" and sturdy. And there is, I think, a formal structure in *Paterson* considerably less arbitrary than Jarrell's com-ments imply. The seasonal motif, as it is related to the plan outlined in the "Author's Note"[16] ("spring, summer, fall and the sea"), is only one of these. But *Paterson's* primary unity is a unity of theme, and it is with this kind of unity that I shall be mainly concerned here.

Before leaving the problem of form, however, I must note an important point raised by Louis Martz in his essay, "The Unicorn in *Paterson:* William Carlos Williams."[17] Martz suggests "that we might regard *Paterson* as a kind of tapestry, woven out of memories and observations, composed by one man's imagination, but written in part by his friends, his patients, and all the milling populace of Paterson, past and present." If such is indeed the case, Jarrell's funda-mental questions are immediately answered. In Williams' poem, just as in a tapestry or mural, particularly a modern tapestry or mural, the arrangement of individual details is not absolutely rigid, and a

14. Cf. *P* 53.
15. *Poetry and the Age* (New York, Knopf, 1953), p. 263.
16. The relevant part reads as follows: "Part One introduces the elemental character of the place. The Second Part comprises the modern replicas. Three will seek a language to make them vocal, and Four, the river below the falls, will be reminiscent of episodes—all that any one man may achieve in a life-time" (*P* 7).
17. In *Thought*, *35*, 543.

certain unavoidable arbitrariness is wholly beside the point. There is a unity of technique which is equally as important as the more conventional unity of structure. Here again, the image of the basket— and its contents—is exactly right: organization may be varied, but the elements are ultimately "gathered up" and assembled into a complex entity.

In both content and form, then, Williams' epic is a "daring" experiment, "a plan for action to supplant a plan for action." The older plan for action is, as abundant internal evidence suggests, the rigid aesthetic theory roughly common to such "learned" and "traditional" poets as Ezra Pound and T. S. Eliot. Williams sees the function of his poem as "a taking up of slack" in art, an ideal which was, of course, related to the program of the Imagists. Williams' celebration of "the ground" is neither derivative nor abstract, and he has been "hard put" to create a poem that is, quite literally, "a reply to Greek and Latin with the bare hands."

Most of the epigraph's remaining phrases refer to Williams' identification of the poem with "a [water]fall." Both, of course, are things of beauty, but in addition Williams sees their functions as similar. That is, each disperses complexity into relative simplicity. The individual particulars thus distinguished may then be "metamorphosed," both as particulars and in new combinations. The dual analytic/synthetic nature of such "metamorphosis" is indicated both in the phrase "by multiplication a reduction to one" and by the single word "resolve." Both poem and falls also permit metamorphosis in the sense of "identification"—either metaphoric identification of one thing *with* another (the "metamorphosis" studied by Sister M. Bernetta Quinn),[18] or identification of one thing *from* another.

After the epigraph comes Williams' "Preface." This begins with a definition of the epic quest followed by the traditional epic question:

> "Rigor of beauty is the quest. But how will you find beauty
> when it is locked in the mind past all remonstrance?"

18. *The Metamorphic Tradition in Modern Poetry* (New Brunswick, N.J., Rutgers University Press, 1955).

The rest of the section answers this question in terms of the themes just introduced in the epigraph:

> To make a start,
> out of particulars
> and make them general, rolling
> up the sum, by defective means—

The means, of course, is the locally oriented poem, the gathering up of dispersed particulars I have already described. Out of such an aggregate, out of such a "rolling up heavy with/ numbers," the poet will ultimately distill the general:[19]

> divided as the dew,
> floating mists, to be rained down and
> regathered into a river that flows
> and encircles.

Such a "means," however, seems to be "defective"—at least to the modern Puritans pursuing the false gods of materialism and traditionalism:

> Sniffing the trees,
> just another dog
> among a lot of dogs. . . .
> The rest have run out—
> after the rabbits.
> Only the lame stands—on
> three legs. Scratch front and back.
> Deceive and eat. Dig
> a musty bone.

Yet a musty bone is better than no bone at all, and in any case, "What/ else is there? And to do?" Moreover, as Williams suggests

19. Cf. 10:4–5.

elsewhere ("Smell!"—*CEP* 153), even the vehicle of his "sniffing" metaphor can serve as a valuable "means" for achieving the goal of his quest.

The main referents of lines 4–5 in the quotation above are, of course, Pound and Eliot—especially Eliot. Williams' reply to Eliot becomes even more overt in the strophes that follow. In a direct paraphrase of the most important line in "East Coker," Williams writes, "For the beginning is *assuredly*/ the end—since we know nothing, pure/ and simple, beyond/ *our own* complexities" (italics mine). In Eliot's poem the whole point is that the statement, "In my beginning is my end," finally gives way to its contrary, despair giving way to hope as the poet invokes a faith that is essentially religious. Williams' wholly secular and humanistic ("local") vision, however, denies both Eliot's "faith" (we may not even understand our own complexities—the sense of "beyond" is highly ambiguous) and the "despair" such "faith" presumably conquers. He affirms that *this* beginning (i.e. *Paterson*) *is* a beginning—indeed, that it is *the* beginning—for only the start made out of particulars can ever lead to fulfillment in the quest for "beauty." There is, in fact, "no return"— no despairing cycle at all. Transcending cycle (through acknowledging it) implies, of course, acceptance of mutability and mortality ("never in this/ world will a man live well in his body/ save dying —and not know himself/ dying; yet that is/ the design"). But unlike Eliot, who seems to despair that his work has been merely a series of futile starts and stops with no real progression, Williams rejoices optimistically (perhaps a bit too optimistically at this point) that his quest will be fulfilled: he has found the means—in an inclusive love —of achieving harmony:

> rolling up out of chaos,
> a nine months' wonder, the city
> the man, an identity—it can't be
> otherwise—an
> interpenetration, both ways. Rolling
> up! obverse, reverse;

> the drunk the sober; the illustrious
> the gross; one.[20]

In his "ignorance" Williams thus possesses "a certain knowledge," definite, though the word is tentative and ambiguous: "Knowledge,/ undispersed"—that is, stale knowledge—is "its own undoing." For then the various potential of "The multiple seed,/ packed tight with detail," "sours" and "is lost in the flux and the mind,/ distracted, floats off in the same/ scum," "and the craft" of poetry is "subverted by thought, rolling up." The poet, therefore, must

> beware lest he turn to no more than
> the writing of stale poems   .   .   .
> Minds like beds always made up,
>   (more stony than a shore)
> unwilling or unable.

The conclusion of the "Preface" brings us to the verge of the epic itself:

> Rolling in, top up,
> under, thrust and recoil, a great clatter:
> lifted as air, boated, multicolored, a
> wash of seas—
> from mathematics to particulars . . .
>
> shells and animalcules
> generally and so to man,
>
> to Paterson.

20. Cf. 245:14.

1.

The Delineaments of the Giants:

PATERSON,
BOOK
ONE

Williams begins his description of "the elemental character of
the place" by introducing the poem's epic protagonist:

> Paterson lies in the valley under the Passaic Falls
> its spent waters forming the outline of his back. He
> lies on his right side, head near the thunder
> of the waters filling his dreams! Eternally asleep,
> his dreams walk about the city where he persists
> incognito. Butterflies settle on his stone ear.
> Immortal he neither moves nor rouses and is seldom
> seen, though be breathes and the subtleties of his
>   machinations
> drawing their substance from the noise of the pouring
>   river
> animate a thousand automatons. Who because they
> neither know their sources nor the sills of their
> disappointments walk outside their bodies aimlessly
>   for the most part,
> locked and forgot in their desires—unroused.

Williams conceives Paterson as a mythic being—a "Giant" somewhat like one of Blake's "Giant Forms"—in whom the qualities of both man and city are fused: "a nine months' wonder, the city/ the man, an identity . . . an/ interpenetration, both ways" (12:5–8). In the prefatory "Author's Note" Williams describes the first half of this equation as follows: "a man in himself is a city, beginning, seeking, achieving and concluding his life in ways which the various aspects of a city may embody—if imaginatively conceived—any city, all the details of which may be made to voice his most intimate convictions." The city is, of course, Paterson, New Jersey, a decidedly working-class, industrial town situated on the Passaic River at the point where the river descends over the Passaic Falls before flowing on to the sea.[1] From what I have said in my introduction, however, it should be obvious that Paterson is also a kind of "anycity" (Williams originally subtitled the poem "Any/Every Place"),[2] important in itself only because it happens to be local to the poet. The "man" involved in Williams' mythic Giant is somewhat more complex. On one level he is a "real" person, Noah Faitoute Paterson. As the name suggests, he is meant to embody, among other things, the Biblical Noah's capacity to survive the Flood (especially important in Book III), Noah Webster's mastery of the American idiom, and the vitally active man's desire to "do all." In a larger sense, then, Paterson is a symbolic personage representing a kind of superior man—Any Man, perhaps, but Every Man only potentially—human, not without flaw, yet embodying a great many powers and desires that Williams finds admirable. Thus, on yet another level, Paterson is a projection of Williams himself (often as "Dr. P."), and it is almost impossible constantly to separate the "poet" and the "persona(e)."

In the lines which open the first section of Book I, Paterson is presented as the animating force of his world: as city, he is the provider of energy and goods, and as man, a kind of mythic myth-

1. See Vivienne Koch, *William Carlos Williams* (Norfolk, Conn., New Directions, 1950), p. 116.
2. Wagner, *The Poems of William Carlos Williams,* p. 113.

maker that bestows life upon his imaginatively created "dreams." ("His machinations," to be sure, draw "their substance from the noise of the pouring river," but, as we shall see, the Falls, especially as a symbol for the local present apotheosized by the loving imagination, is ultimately mythicized as an aspect of the protagonist.) Yet to the machines and machine-men who cannot feel his power, Paterson seems to be "asleep"—that is, asleep as *they* are asleep, "locked and forgot in their desires—unroused." They cannot recognize Paterson's "immortality,"[3] and like Blake's fragmented, fallen men, they wander about without hope or faith, separated from both their physical bodies and their imaginative beings.

As we might expect, Williams' myth in *Paterson* requires, as the complement to the male principle, a "supplying female" that the poet must "marry." The "female to the city" is, of course, the natural landscape in which the city is located—the Valley of the Rocks and Garrett Mountain Park:

> And there, against him, stretches the low mountain.
> The Park's her head, carved, above the Falls, by the quiet
> river . . .
>   facing him, his
> arm supporting her, by the *Valley of the Rocks,* asleep.
> Pearls at her ankles, her monstrous hair
> spangled with apple-blossoms is scattered about into
> the back country, waking their dreams.

Ultimately, however, the city's relation to its landscape is emblematic of man's relation to his world, and it is primarily the latter which *Paterson* is "about." The "secret of those rocks," therefore, is the "colored crystals . . . farms and ponds, laurel and the temperate wild

---

3. An "immortality" associated, as my later discussion will make clear, with the "immortality" of the "eternal moment," and hence of individual works of art ("stone" becomes especially important in *Paterson* II) and of art in general. Note, however, that Paterson does "breathe."

cactus,/ yellow flowered"—which man both discovers and creates.[4]
As at the end of Wallace Stevens' *Sunday Morning,* where

> Deer walk upon our mountains, and the quail
> Whistle about us their spontaneous cries;
> Sweet berries ripen in the wilderness;
> And, in the isolation of the sky,
> At evening, casual flocks of pigeons make
> Ambiguous undulations as they sink,
> Downward to darkness, on extended wings

—so here

> . . . the deer run
> and the wood-duck nests protecting his gallant plumage.

It is the particulars of common reality that are most valuable. The
world outside the city ("nature") is a part of the world outside the
man ("reality"), but it should be emphasized that it is only a part.
The reality external to the self, out of which the artist's love and
imagination bring "art" into being, also includes the city ("artifacts").
Indeed, as we shall see apropos of Book III, "cities" thus viewed become incorporated into ("a part of") an expanded definition of
"nature."

As the meeting point between male and female, the Passaic River
is the master image in the poem—indeed, it is the master image
of the poem. It symbolizes so many things that its full significance
becomes apparent only as the poem develops, but many of its most
important meanings can be understood from the start. Most simply,
it is a more or less objective representation of a particular city and,
more importantly, of a particular man. As Williams puts it in a news
release dated May 31, 1951,[5] "the course of the river . . . seemed

4. Cf. *Portrait of a Lady, CEP* 40.
5. Entitled "News from New Directions." The pertinent section is headed
"A Statement by William Carlos Williams About the Poem *Paterson.*" I wish

more and more to resemble my own life as I more and more thought of it: the river above the Falls, the catastrophe of the Falls itself, the river below the Falls, and the entrance at the end into the great sea." More generally, however, the river is a symbol of the life of "Paterson"—the life of Any Man and, potentially, even of Every Man—a symbol of the stream of human experience, historically and mythically considered, which is the historic side of the myth Williams presents in *In the American Grain.* On yet another level the river symbolizes Paterson's (or Williams') stream of consciousness, the flow of thought which emerges out of memory and vanishes into the mind's dim sense of "infinity." Thus the lines with which the poet introduces this symbol:

> From above, higher than the spires, higher
> even than the office towers, from oozy fields
> abandoned to grey beds of dead grass,
> black sumac, withered weed-stalks,
> mud and thickets cluttered with dead leaves—
> the river comes pouring in above the city
> and crashes from the edge of the gorge
> in a recoil of spray and rainbow mists.

In some sense at least, Williams views his river as something almost divine, above the religions of convention, above even the appropriative, materialistic religions of today.

The last three lines here present the river's most important aspect. The image is developed in the extraordinary passage that follows:

> Jostled as are the waters approaching
> the brink, his thoughts
> interlace, repel and cut under,
> rise rock-thwarted and turn aside
> but forever strain forward . . .

---

to thank Louis L. Martz, Douglas Tracy Smith Professor of English and American Literature, Yale University, for supplying me with this item.

            . . . they coalesce now
    glass-smooth with their swiftness,
    quiet or seem to quiet as at the close
    they leap to the conclusion and
    fall, fall in air! as if
    floating, relieved of their weight,
    split apart, ribbons; dazed, drunk
    with the catastrophe of the descent
    floating unsupported
    to hit the rocks: to a thunder,
    as if lightning had struck

    All lightness lost, weight regained in
    the repulse, a fury of
    escape driving them to rebound
    upon those coming after—
    keeping nevertheless to the stream, they
    retake their course, the air full
    of the tumult and of spray
    connotative of the equal air, coeval,
    filling the void.

The Falls, as these lines indicate, is not conceived simply as falling: it is static as well as kinetic,[6] and it appears to rise as well as descend.[7] Such motionless motion is primarily important in regard to what might be called the "eternal moment," the "moment of moments," or the "moment of the eternal present." This concept is not at all peculiar to Williams, and is in fact one of the important concepts common to virtually all modern writers.

One source of the idea is perhaps to be found in Blake. At the end of the first Book of *Milton* he characterizes poetic time as follows:

6. Cf. the Simplon Pass passage in Book VI of Wordsworth's *Prelude* (l. 626).
7. Cf. 119:5–9.

Every Time less than a pulsation of the artery
Is equal in its period & value to Six Thousand Years.
For in this Period the Poet's Work is Done, and all the Great
Events of Time start forth & are conceiv'd in such a Period,
Within a Moment, a Pulsation of the Artery.

Pater, from whom most modern versions of this theme have been derived in one way or another, presents a similar idea in the famous Conclusion to his *Studies in the History of the Renaissance:*

> we are all under sentence of death but with a sort of indefinite reprieve . . . we have an interval, and then our place knows us no more. . . . our one chance lies in expanding that interval, in getting as many pulsations as possible into the given time. Great passions may give us this quickened sense of life . . . Only be sure it is passion—that it does yield you this fruit of a quickened, multipled consciousness. Of such wisdom, the poetic passion, the desire of beauty, the love of art for its own sake, has most. For art comes to you proposing frankly to give nothing but the highest quality to your moments as they pass, and simply for those moments' sake.

"The moment" is described by Yeats as the point where "The Zodiac [gyres] is changed into a sphere" *(Chosen);* by Joyce as "the moment the focus is reached [and] the object is epiphanized" *(Stephen Hero);* by Eliot as "the still point of the turning world," where time intersects with the timeless *(Four Quartets);* by Pound as the "instant of time" in which the "intellectual and emotional complex" which is the "image" is "presented" *(A Few Don'ts by an Imagist);* and by D. H. Lawrence as a moment, often violently sexual, "at the core of space/ at the quick/ of time" *(Swan)*. This moment in which past, present, and future are all rolled into one—or, to use another frame of reference, in which the reality of the present is apotheosized[8]—figures as a crucial basis of all Williams' poetry. As he puts

8. See 172:10–173:11, 237:20–238:3.

it in his review of Byron Vazakas' *Transfigured Night,* "No world can exist for more than the consuming of a match or the eating of an apple without a poet to breathe into it an immortality."[9] Or, as we read in the brilliantly paradoxical conclusion to *Shadows* (PB 150–52),[10]

> The instant
> trivial as it is
> is all we have
> unless—unless
> things the imagination feeds upon,
> the scent of the rose,
> startle us anew.

The poet, that is, has the power "to refine, to clarify, to intensify that eternal moment in which we alone live."[11] In the description of the Falls, both past and future imaginatively become one with the present—a present whose beauty is eternal even as it is ephemeral. Since the Falls, finally, is a symbol of the "descent" (dispersal and metamorphosis) as this applies to creative art and to creative life, it is this "catastrophe"—i.e. "downturning" (cf. ambiguity of "fall") —that is ultimately affirmed as "immortal."

I allude to the phrase from the epigraph, "a dispersal and a metamorphosis," purposefully. For together with the meanings just discussed, the Falls also represents the power of the loving and imaginative poet to localize and clarify particulars. As the Falls "combs out"

9. "Preface," *Quarterly Review of Literature,* 2, 348. The poet, Williams goes on to say, "seems more the artist, the poet in the full sense of a transformer by the work of the imagination, than anyone I know. . . . Like the newspaper that takes things as it finds them—mutilated and deformed, but drops what it finds as it was, unchanged in all its deformity and mutilation— the poet, challenging the event, recreates it as of whence it sprang from among men and women, and makes a new world of it" (cf. P 120:18–32).

10. Cf. P 278:3–4.

11. *Spring and All* (Dijon, France, Contact Publishing Co., 1923), p. 3.

25

the river, so the poet "combs out" the tangled chaos of experience, separating strand from strand so that each may be apprehended in all its individuality. Compare the poem Williams published separately as *Paterson: The Falls* (*CLP* 10–11):

> (What common language to unravel?
> .   .   combed into straight lines
> from that rafter of a rock's
> lip.)

This image becomes especially important in *Paterson* II.

Apropos of *In the American Grain* I pointed out Williams' enthusiastic response to "natural" (i.e. "visible" or "given") "wonders." Such a response is crucial in *Paterson,* and indeed the realm of the "wonderful" is the source of virtually all its most important sections. Tellingly, then, the Falls (and all it represents) is proclaimed "A wonder! A wonder!", just as in the earlier prose work the New World is proclaimed "the greatest wonder in the world." To emphasize the point, Williams weaves the rest of the section out of a number of other "wonders." The first of these is the "exciting" discovery of pearls in Notch Brook. The episode comes just after the description of the secret of the Park's rocks, the "Pearls at her ankles," and the pearls found hidden in the brook are clearly an example of the beauty freely given by the natural world. Yet, as the remainder of this passage suggests, the "Puritan" impulse toward appropriation immediately corrupts any possibility of a more loving and imaginative response, and the search for beauty is consequently unfulfilled.

Williams now restates his mythic tenet that Paterson is the source of life in his world:

> . . . Mr.
> Paterson has gone away
> to rest and write. Inside the bus one sees
> his thoughts sitting and standing. His
> thoughts alight and scatter . . .

26

           . . . that they may live
his thought is listed in the Telephone
Directory.

And in an unjustifiably vulgar, yet I think serious, aside, the poet
also makes his giant the source of the Falls: "And derivatively, for
the Great Falls,/ PISS-AGH! the giant lets fly!" Such things as these,
and especially such things as they metaphorically and symbolically
represent (i.e. the power of "poetic" creation in art and life), are
themselves wonders—related, albeit tenuously, to Moses' "wonderful" vision of the promised land (Deut. 34:1-4).

The next wonder is "a dwarf, hideously deformed," "a monster in
human form." This creature, half man, half vegetable, reappears
in *Paterson* II as a symbol of the faithless and unwary poet's possible
fate, of an "actual" defeat.[12] On another level, however, it also
suggests possible failures in interpretation. When a poet ("wonder")
becomes a freak, either he has failed to maintain faith in himself,
or others have failed to approach him with love and imagination (cf.
the "gentleman" who sees both the dwarf and the Falls merely as
"natural curiosit[ies] then existing in the community"[13]). This
latter attitude is very close to the appropriative attitude maintained
by the pearl-hunters toward the pearls—and indeed both attitudes
come together in the final episode of this sequence, "The Monster
Taken."[14]

The failure to respond generously to the world's natural wonders
is the failure to "marry," and it leads only to "divorce"—or, what is
the same thing, to the fearful or appropriative attitude which is a
"marriage only to destroy." The poet makes this clear in the sequence of lyrics and prose items which follows. The first lyric is
especially important:

12. Cf. 101:25–102:10 and ff.
13. Remarks that Williams was at most a poet of some local significance
hurt the poet deeply.
14. Cf. 64:15–65:7.

> They begin!
> The perfections are sharpened
> The flower spreads its colored petals
> wide in the sun
> But the tongue of the bee
> misses them
> They sink back into the loam
> crying out
> —you may call it a cry
> that creeps over them, a shiver
> as they wilt and disappear:
> Marriage come to have a shuddering
> implication...
>
> The language is missing them
> they die also
> incommunicado.

The image of flowers (plural since the things of the world are plural) is introduced at almost the beginning of the poem:[15] "A man like a city and a woman like a flower/ —who are in love. Two women. Three women./ Innumerable women, each like a flower./ But/ only one man—like a city." In the lyric here, however, vitalizing love of the world is unconsummated. The language of love—that is, the language of poetry, of truth, of the local[16]—is unlearned and unused. The end of such marriageless marriage is the "shuddering implication" only of death.[17] Yet as the prose passage which follows (an account of the so-called "Jackson's Whites," and of the innumerable desecrated women who bore them) emphasizes, much of the modern world *is* a world of divorce, with sources to be found in the violence, lust, and greed of the past.

15. Cf. *Asphodel, That Greeny Flower* (PB, esp. pp. 151, 153).
16. Compare lines 21:2–6 with 237:11–238:3 and with the first sentence on p. 226 of *In the American Grain.*
17. Cf. 129:20–131:7 and my first epigraph.

That it need not be so, however, Williams suggests in the next passage:

> I remember
> a *Geographic* picture, the 9 women
> of some African chief semi-naked
> astraddle a log, an official log to
> be presumed, heads left:
>
> Foremost
> froze the young and latest,
> erect, a proud queen, conscious of her power,
> mud-caked, her monumental hair
> slanted above the brows—violently frowning.
>
> Behind her, packed tight up
> in a descending scale of freshness
> stiffened the others
>
> and then   .   .
> the last, the first wife,
> present! supporting all the rest growing
> up from her—whose careworn eyes
> serious, menacing—but unabashed; breasts
> sagging from hard use   .   .
>
> Whereas the uppointed breasts
> of that other, tense, charged with
> pressures unrelieved   .
> and the rekindling they bespoke
> was evident.

The beauty here, the vitality, the manifest sexuality—all attest to a triumph of human love, a triumph of the mutual relationship of marriage. The African chief, the poet, and even the *Geographic* photographer give generously to these nine wives their love and imaginative trust; and they are rewarded in turn by the freely given fruits of exuberant beauty. Such a marriage, as we shall see, is "a marriage that stares death in the eye," defeating it "eternally." This is imaged particularly in the "first wife," who, even though old and near physical death (hence the careworn, serious eyes), is as proud and conscious of her power (she "all of a piece, holds up the others") as is the ninth, most recent wife.[18]

Williams ends Section I with the accounts of two different people who made, quite literally, the "descent" into the Passaic Falls. The episodes emphasize, on one level, man's need for vital, loving, and imaginative "language"; on another level, the possibility that descent, especially if misunderstood, can be perilous; and on still another level, that the vertigo-producing power of the Falls can itself be dangerous. The first episode centers upon one "Mrs. Sarah Cumming, consort of the Rev. Hopper Cumming, of Newark," who, while observing with her husband "the wonderful prospect, and making various remarks upon the stupendous works of nature around them," fell or leaped (Williams later implies that he believes the latter) "into the fatal flood." We are not told why, but if the sentimental description of this two-month bride's "Temporal felicity and usefulness" is any index to her "life," the explanation seems rather obvious. If she did jump toward what she considered Life, however,[19] she misinterpreted the pouring language of the Falls, for the voice of

18. About this passage Vivienne Koch has written that "the contrast between the leveling and barren present and the fecundity of a primitive society, graded in terms of natural vitality, is established by juxtaposing the African women to the girls from 'decayed families,'" and that "the tragic descent in scale and function is undeniable" (*Williams,* p. 124). But if this applies, at least for the most part, to the contrast between past and present, it does not apply to the sequence of wives on the log, and it therefore seems to me that the implications of the passage are not altogether tragic.

19. She does, I think, see the Falls as a "wonder" rather than as a "curiosity." It is also significant that her understanding of "homeward" is very much akin to Boone's, Poe's, and Paterson/Williams', while her husband's is just the opposite.

the Falls, however attractive in itself, ultimately teaches *reconciliation* with our world—the true meaning of "descent."

The second episode describes the descents made by Sam Patch, "then a resident in Paterson, who was a boss over cotton spinners in one of the mills." Patch's career began with a successful leap from the edge of the Passaic Falls, when he dived after a fallen pin that was being used to place a new bridge into position. Although he had frequently announced that he would perform such a feat, the actual jump seems to have been more or less spontaneous. As a manifestation of both local pride and daring energy, it is a symbol of the descent that Williams continually affirms. It is particularly important that Patch's language, and the language of the teller of his "GRRRREAT HISTORY" (one of the men under him in the mill), is thoroughly vital and local ("These were the words that Sam Patch said: 'Now, old Tim Crane[20] thinks he has done something great; but I can beat him.'"). As a result of his jump, Patch became a local, even national "marvel," and he "toured the country/ diving from cliffs and masts, rocks and bridges." Yet his career suddenly ended when he failed to come up after an unsuccessful dive from Genesee Falls in Rochester, New York: "Instead of descending with a plummet-like fall his body wavered in the air . . . He struck the water on his side and disappeared. . . . Not until the following spring was the body found frozen in an ice-cake." The reasons for his failure are manifest. In the first place, he had left his native territory. More importantly, however, he had gradually made his diving into a means—of fame, self-aggrandizement— rather than an end. Thus, "Speech had failed him. He was confused. The word had been drained of its meaning."

In Book I, Section II, the poet sustains a lengthy meditation on the validity of the themes and techniques he has introduced in Section I. This section is highly personal, and, as we would expect in a meditation, essentially argumentative—often even a kind of dialogue

20. One cannot help but think, at this point, of another bridge-builder, Hart Crane.

with an interior questioning voice. It begins in a tone of despair curiously mixed with a kind of confidence:

> There is no direction. Whither? I
> cannot say. I cannot say
> more than how. The how (the howl) only
> is at my disposal (proposal) : watching—
> colder than stone   .

As we have seen, the poet frankly admits his quest is a "daring" one; where it will lead is altogether unknown. Yet he is not entirely lost, for at the very least he has a "plan for action." This may seem merely an impractical absurdity to "others"—at times, perhaps, even to himself—but he remains hopefully "watching" nonetheless.

The world which he watches, however, is "colder than stone,"

> a bud forever green,
> tight-curled, upon the pavement, perfect
> in juice and substance but divorced, divorced
> from its fellows, fallen low.

A few pages later the poet identifies this bud of eternally unripened potential specifically as "the university," a symbol of the "divorce [which] is/ the sign of knowledge in our time"—man's divorce from his world, his fellows, the "language." Stagnating tradition and restraint have created a world of "unfledged desire, irresponsible, green," "unready" to flower into the fulfillment of imagination and love, and hence a stifling "challenge" to possible rebirth. It is important to note, however, that here the bud may also be a symbol of the artist in isolation, attempting with only partial success to induce the "sleep and silence" not of fear or death but rather of imagination.[21]

21. As we shall see, "sleep" and "silence" both have multiple meanings in the poem, and "the roar of the river" may be either the oppressive din of "the library" (cf. III, i) or the roar of the pouring waters of the present (cf. 172:10 ff.).

This secondary meaning is subtly developed in a poignantly beautiful but tightly controlled description of "Two halfgrown girls hailing hallowed Easter." They are associated with the Falls, and hence with the poet, by "the pouring/ waters of their hair," as well as by the "ribbons" (cf. 16:20) that gather and order it.[22] But one holds a "gathered spray" (another allusion to the Falls) from a *"leafless* bush in full *bud"* (italics mine), able only to "stroke the soft fur" and comment, in what Jarrell has perfectly expressed as a "touching half-success, half-failure of language"[23]: "Ain't they beautiful!" Both the action[24] and the language indicate the possibility of and "instinct" toward human flowering, but the two girls are only "halfgrown" and *their* Easter must await the future. The latent but uncomprehended sexuality of the reference to "eels or a moon" lends further support to this reading.

As the poet continues to meditate, he comes to realize *why* there is no fixed direction to his quest: he is "not a robin nor erudite,/ no Erasmus nor bird that returns to the same/ ground year by year"— that is, no tradition-bound academician. To be sure, he remains grounded in the local, but his relation to it changes as the ground itself undergoes subtle transformations, "its identity altered." His relation to his ground must change, for the poet's task is a metamorphosing unification of dispersed particulars, a continual making of new poems:

> .   .   a mass of detail
> to interrelate on a new ground, difficultly;
> an assonance, a homologue
> > triple piled
> pulling the disparate together to clarify
> and compress.

22. Just as the combed-out strands of "the poem" effect an artful gathering and ordering of the "Falls" of thought and experience.
23. "The Poet and his Public," p. 495.
24. Cf. 69:3–10.

Yet if the "theme," like the poet, may prove "asleep, unrecognized—/ all of a piece, alone/ in a wind that does not move the others," if the "Whither" is not precisely known, at least the "How" and "Whence" are obvious: "a way to spend/ a Sunday afternoon while the green bush shakes"—or, as one can see in retrospect after reading *Paterson* II ("Sunday in the Park"), the "way" of imaginative, loving marriage in a vital, eternal present (symbolized here by the quivering, but locally rooted, juniper).

In spite of the clarification the poet has achieved, thoughts of despair and suicide, apparently not uncommon, suddenly return to trouble him: beauty seems an illusion "where there is none/ or none available," and life itself ("breath") seems "Stale as a whale's breath." He recalls the deaths of Sam Patch and Mrs. Cumming (distinguishing with bitter irony the "leap" of the former from the "fall" of the latter), reflecting that they were "both silent, uncommunicative" and implying that the same may also be true of himself. Rehabilitating thoughts, however, soon follow, and the poet more or less reestablishes mental equilibrium:

> Only of late, late! begun to know, to
> know clearly (as through clear ice) whence
> I draw my breath or how to employ it
> clearly—if not well . . .
>
> —and watch, wrapt! one branch
> of the tree at the fall's edge, one
> mottled branch, withheld,
> among the gyrate branches
> of the waist-thick sycamore,
> sway less, among the rest, separate, slowly
> with giraffish awkwardness, slightly
> on a long axis, so slightly
> as hardly to be noticed, in itself the tempest:

Thus

the first wife, with giraffish awkwardness . . .

34

        on a log, her varnished hair
trussed up like a termite's nest (forming
the lines) and, her old thighs
gripping the log reverently, that,
all of a piece, holds up the others—
alert.

Whence he draws his breath, to employ it "clearly" if "awkwardly,"[25] is "certainly NOT the university," the seat of past tradition whose breath has long since gone stale. It is rather the vitality of the local present embodied in the adverbial phrase "While the green bush sways," the "eternal moment" that transcends all fear of death and in harmony with which the poet himself sways, "all of a piece." There is, then, a "source"—symbolized by the "first wife," the "first beauty," the "flower within a flower"—whose "history" lives forever "within the mind" (in "its den in the rock" behind the Falls) and "laughs at the names/ by which they [academicians, the "others"] think to trap it." Such a source is "not for the sake of the encyclopedia," but for the ever-living life of the imagination.

Paterson's meditation now becomes even more an attack on learning and its absurd pretenses:

        the whole din of fracturing thought
        as it falls tinnily to nothing upon the streets . . .

                Pithy philosophies of
        daily exits and entrances, with books
        propping up one end of the shaky table—
        The vague accuracies of events dancing two
        and two with language which they
        forever surpass—and dawns
        tangled in darkness.

This attack in turn modulates into the thoughts of a frustrated lover (presumably Paterson himself)[26] as he sits by the Falls with a

25. At least in comparison with Nature. See 31:17–19.
26. See the "Phyllis & Paterson" dialogues in IV, i.

reticent mistress. He has "much to say," but it can be said only in the wordless language of love. The lovers "sit and talk, sensing *a little*/ the rushing impact of the giants'/ violent torrent rolling over [them], *a/ few moments*" (italics mine), but the flower of fulfillment remains closed, a bud of "unacknowledged desire." "The language" is denied, the "source" is ignored, and the air "brings in the rumors of separate/ worlds" only. Yet even so, the center of this passage remains the celebration of an imaginative love in an infinitely expanded interval:[27]

> . . . to
> go to bed with you, to pass beyond
> the moment of meeting, while the
> currents float still in mid-air, to
> fall—
> with you from the brink, before
> the crash—

> to seize the moment.

To be sure, this celebration of marriage is precarious, as emphasized by the examples of "divorced" human beings which follow: "Billie" (shockingly, a type far from unique: "I told my buddie, in Hartford, she was just like our landlady, THE PISTOL. He said he had a sister just like that"), the person afraid of being murdered, the woman with the new set of artificial teeth,[28] the yelping dog,[29] "a great belly/ that no longer laughs but mourns/ with its expressionless black navel love's/ deceit." But from these the poet detaches himself: "They fail, they limp with corns. . . . They are the divisions and imbalances/ of his whole concept, made weak by pity,/ flouting desire." The poem seems to be falling apart (as the poet

27. Cf. 16:4–17:4.
28. Cf. *The Waste Land,* second section.
29. Cf. 157:5–159:19.

admits by beginning a new section), but the rigors of his meditation have at least helped to clarify his position. Thus a correspondent identified as "E. D."[30] implores him "to submit to your own myths" and to bridge the gap that so easily arises between literature ("the book") and life ("the man"). Such abstract advice is easy enough to give, of course, but the poet continues his struggle to follow it, continues unrelentingly to pursue his unfamiliar and difficult course:

> A delirium of solutions, forthwith, forces
> him into back streets, to begin again:
> up hollow stairs among acrid smells
> to obscene rendezvous.

The new start the poet makes in Section III, then, has its impetus in a reconciling confrontation of fragmentation and decay. In the opening lines the poet faces directly the "fact" that the world of the present is, in general, a world of denial in which the flowering of imagination and love is partial at best:

> How strange you are, you idiot!
> So you think because the rose
> is red that you shall have the mastery?
> The rose is green and will bloom,
> overtopping you, green, livid
> green when you shall no more speak, or
> taste, or even be.

Yet if the world of the present—that is, the "rose"—is "livid green," at least it *is* a rose rather than a bud. To the imaginative and loving poet (in each of us) who is generous and trusting enough to "marry" such a world, beauty *is* available.

This becomes strikingly clear in the lyrical meditation that follows. Paterson is standing by a window. Melting snow is dripping from

30. "T. J." in the original edition (1946).

the cornice outside at "90 strokes a minute," imaging once again the association between the poet's thoughts and imaginings and the Falls. The phrase "90 strokes a minute" also seems to refer to the pulsations of the poet's heart, for he is clearly in a state of heightened consciousness. Most important, however, are the lines, "He picked a hairpin from the floor/ and stuck it in his ear, probing/ around inside." To be sure, this is a disgusting, even unjustifiable, image, yet if it is radical, so is the poet's situation,[31] and the image's shocking rigor does save the subsequent affirmations from facile charges of sentimentality. In any case, the poet's daring here leads to a truly magnificent fulfillment, for in a concrete particular of his local world he perceives a visionary confirmation of the marriage that is the goal of his quest:

> He descried
> in the linoleum at his feet a woman's
> face.

The poet resides in his world in a state of almost total poverty (in Stevens' sense), but that world still responds to his imaginative generosity by returning an image of the beauty both created and discovered by their marriage. The perception of metaphorical and symbolical relationships, which is of course the sign of the active imagination, continues as the poet descries in the rolling of "his thumb/ about the tip of his left index finger . . . the head/ of a cat licking its paw" (itself an image closely akin to the "combing" image discussed above). Then the passage reaches its Blakean climax, and the pessimism born of world-knowledge becomes itself an optimism ultimately merging with the optimism born of self-knowledge and delight:[32]

---

31. "Searching the punk dry rot for beauty." Note that it is "of/ earth his ears are full."

32. I have here paraphrased a sentence from Vivienne Koch (*Williams*, p. 131).

: And his thoughts soared
to the magnificence of imagined delights
where he would probe

as into the pupil of an eye
as through a hoople of fire, and emerge
sheathed in a robe

streaming with light. What heroic
dawn of desire
is denied to his thoughts?

They are trees
from whose leaves streaming with rain
his mind drinks of desire.

The paradoxical use of the word "probe" at this point unites the beginning of the section with its end, ensuring that both heat and light are begotten by the poet's imagination and love.

At this point the sequence is interrupted by a brief—and I think unsuccessful—lyric, still on the subject of the decay of beauty and freshness. The persona involved is as much Paterson the city as Paterson the man. After questioning the value of the "youth" of "the contemptible twig" (Nature? the idyllic past?), he comes to the conclusion that even in his decline he surpasses "youth's leanness":

I enclose it and
     persist, go on. . . .

My surface is myself.
     Under which
to witness, youth is
     buried. Roots?

Everybody has roots.

After this interruption, the triplet sequence concludes, with lines which again repudiate "the university": "what they publish/ severally or as a group: clerks/ got out of hand forgetting for the most part/ to whom they are beholden." Unlike "poets," who manage to "go on living" because they, even while intensely aware of their sources, continually readjust to the world as it is, the members of the academy are "spitted on fixed concepts like/ roasting hogs, sputtering, their drip sizzling/ in the fire." Their "something else" repeatedly turns out to be merely "something else the same."

The various instances of divorce pointed up by several brief sketches which follow—the description of a young colored girl refused a baby; the contrast between the sterile luxury enjoyed, "in time of general privation," by a wealthy country gentleman, and the variety, abundance, and order to be found in the seemingly paltry estate of Cornelius Doremus—lead Williams to comment further on the sources of such divorce, on the restriction of humane "knowledge." "Some say/ it is the decay of the middle class/ making an impossible moat between the high/ and the low where/ the life once flourished." Yet as we shall see, even "among/ the working classes SOME sort/ of breakdown/ has occurred," so if free intercourse between the sources of light and heat has ceased because of a "decay of the middle class," this is only a part of a more general cause. This brings the poet back to the unimaginative, loveless, tradition-bound individuals symbolized by "the knowledgeable idiots, the university." If they, too, are only partly to blame, their responsibility is nevertheless greater: "they at least are the non-purveyors/ should be devising means/ to leap the gap. . . . They block the release/ that should cleanse and assume/ prerogatives as a private recompense." In the final analysis, however, Williams generalizes even more by admitting that "Others are also at fault because/ they do nothing."

As the section nears its conclusion, the poet thinks once more of "the men that ran/ and could run off/ toward the peripheries—/ to other centers, direct—/ for clarity (if/ they found it)/ loveliness and/ authority in the world"—that is, of the expatriates, especially

Pound and Eliot. But to Williams the eclectic traditionalism they sought is illusory. He insists that the "sort of springtime/ toward which their minds aspired" is to be found only in the local, only in the "fertile mud"—to refer again to the prose passage just before— into which imaginative man is willing to "descend." Thus a reminiscence of Sam Patch and a brief prose item describing a dead body found "hanging over the precipice" of the Falls bring the poet back to the present. He again confronts its decay and sordidness directly, finding a kind of beauty as he does so:

> Half the river bed, half steaming purple
> from the factory vents, spewed out hot,
> swirling, bubbling. The dead bank,
> shining mud[33] . . .
>
> And silk spins from the hot drums to a music
> of pathetic souvenirs, a comb and nail-file
> in an imitation leather case—to
> remind him, to remind him! and
> a photograph-holder with pictures of himself
> between the two children, all returned
> weeping, weeping.

The beauty of the "ground" is not, of course, the more traditional beauty of the "finished product," but Williams is perfectly aware of this and wryly counters an imagined objection from his friend Pound as follows:

> P. Your interest is in the bloody loam but what
> I'm after is the finished product.
>
> I. Leadership passes into empire; empire begets in-
> solence; insolence brings ruin.

33. Cf. *The Rime of the Ancient Mariner*, 11.263–91.

41

Williams realizes that his kind of beauty may never be as sculptured and ordered as the beauty of the totally finished product (if, indeed, such can ever exist), but at the very least it will always be fresh and varied. "And so among the rest he drives/ in his new car out to the suburbs, out/ by the rhubarb farm—a simple thought—/ where the convent of the Little Sisters of/ St. Ann pretends a mystery." Confidently, purposefully, the poet details the scene before him. Then, as he observes with a mixture of love and pity, he quietly summarizes his imaginative faith:

> . . . have here
> their forthright beauty, beside:
>
> Things, things unmentionable,
> the sink with the waste farina in it and
> lumps of rancid meat, milk-bottle-tops: have
> here a tranquility and loveliness
> Have here (in his thoughts)
> a complement tranquil and chaste.

This is what Wallace Stevens, in *Of Modern Poetry,* calls "the poem of the mind in the act of finding/ What will suffice."[34] Williams, perhaps, is here a bit more insistent than Stevens that he has indeed found what will suffice, but to both poets the act of finding itself is ultimately most important. This is particularly emphasized in the poetry with which the section ends:

> Thought clambers up,
> snail like, upon the wet rocks
> hidden from sun and sight—
> hedged in by the pouring torrent—
> and has its birth and death there

34. This part of *Paterson* also has marked affinities with Stevens' *The Man on the Dump.*

in that moist chamber, shut from
the world—and unknown to the world,
cloaks itself in mystery—

                       And the myth
that holds up the rock,
that holds up the water thrives there—
in that cavern, that profound cleft,
                a flickering green
inspiring terror, watching   .   .

And standing, shrouded there, in that din,
Earth, the chatterer, father of all
speech   .   .   .   .

We have already seen what this myth is: Paterson/Williams' faith
that meaning is to be found only in imaginative and loving marriage
with the things of the local world. Such a myth is of course the
ultimate meaning of the Falls, and it is not only the source but also
the end of the poet's quest.

2.

Sunday in the Park:

PATERSON, BOOK TWO

A WORLD WHICH I APPROACH CONCRETELY

The opening few lines of Book II state once more *Paterson's* major theme:

> Outside
>
>   outside myself
>
>   there is a world,
>   he rumbled, subject to my incursions
>   —a world
>   (to me) at rest
>   which I approach
>   concretely.

The "he" here is of course the poem's epic protagonist. Since "Paterson" is both city and man, the terms "Outside" and "outside myself" mean both "out of the town" and "out of the self": both "parks" are "females to the city," as I have already suggested. The relationship between man and reality, the "approach" to or "love" of his world by man, is precisely the kind of relationship I have described as a "marriage." It is enormously involved with non-appropriative aesthetic apprehension. This is not contradicted by the phrase "subject to my incursions" in the fourth line. To be sure, an "incursion" suggests pragmatic, use-oriented "Puritanism," but as the line stands, the world is only "subject" to such violation.[1] As with any marriage, the relationship is constantly threatened by the possibility of mere appropriation, but although the threat is inevitable, its materialization is not. At any rate, such an "approach" clearly requires a sympathy toward the approached on the part of the approacher, and it is significant that at this point Williams uses a metaphor which derives from classical relativity:[2] a given "world" is "at rest" to an observer only when both are moving in identical fashion with respect to some (arbitrary) fixed standard of reference. The final word of this passage ("concretely") brings Williams' prime aesthetic tenet ("Say it, no ideas but in things"—14:17) to bear on "life." As poetry is meaningful to Williams only when reality (including truth as well as beauty) is presented directly, so life is meaningful only when reality is approached directly. Love and aesthetic fulfillment in life, as well as the "ideas" of poetry, must be rooted in "things."

After this introductory statement of theme, the development of Book II's "plot" begins:

> The scene's the Park
> upon the rock,
> female to the city

> —upon whose body Paterson instructs his thoughts
> (concretely)

> —late spring,
> a Sunday afternoon!

1. Cf. 125:11–34.
2. Cf. the "radiant gist" theme in Books III and IV.

Paterson, primarily as the persona with whom Williams more or less identifies himself, is "out on the mountain,"[3] walking through the Park which is a symbol both of reality and of a potential world of imagination. Like the pastoral world, this world is a place of physical and visionary refreshment, but unlike the pastoral world, it is to be found in the local present: to Williams as to Wallace Stevens, "There is, in fact, a world of poetry indistinguishable from the world in which we live."[4] Upon the concrete particulars of reality, imaginatively conceived, then, the poet is "instructing" his thoughts, "schooling" them in the "DEEtails" upon which the world of the imagination must be "grounded." On the mythic level the Giant Paterson is "in-forming" and revitalizing his thoughts—his dreams, which walk about the city as automatons who do not know their sources (14:5–16)—through his intimate association with the enduring principle of love, imagination, and life embodied by the female.

As Paterson "goes by the footpath to the cliff," he sees the minute particulars of his environment—the landscape:

> Thickets gather about groups of squat sand-pine,
> all but from bare rock   .   .
>
> —a scattering of man-high cedars (sharp cones),
> antlered sumac   .

as well as the city:

>   . . . he,
> looks back (beautiful but expensive!) to
> the pearl-grey towers!   [cf. 17:11–13]

---

3. As Williams puts it in a conversation with John C. Thirlwall, Apr. 8, 1954. See below, p. 65, n. 19.

4. *The Necessary Angel: Essays on Reality and the Imagination* (New York, Knopf, 1951), p. 31; cf. p. 54.

More important, Paterson also sees the human beings who surround him:[5]

>   laughing, calling to each other—
>
>   Wait for me!
>
> .   .   the ugly legs of the young girls,
> pistons too powerful for delicacy!   .
> the men's arms, red, used to heat and cold,
> to toss quartered beeves and   .
>
>   Yah! Yah! Yah! Yah!

These are the distinctly working-class people of Paterson, the local people of the local world. Williams often sees them as an amorphous, decadent, unimaginative mass:

>   Minds beaten thin
>   by waste—among
>
>   the working classes SOME sort
>   of breakdown
>   has occurred.   [66:21–67:3]

As they are cut off from their sources ("roots, for the most part, writhing/ upon the surface"—59:6–9), so are they cut off from their world and from one another ("Divorce is/ the sign of knowledge in our time,/ divorce! divorce!"—28:10–12). Ultimately, however, Williams does come to terms with them; they are a part of his world to which he must ultimately "be reconciled" (cf. 103:11–12). His approach must be made irrespective of any breakdown that may have occurred. If his world is not a world of love, he must remain

5. Cf. *CEP* 7.

"still the positive" to it "in spite of all." Nor is the breakdown complete. At the very least, as Williams' vigorous verse intimates, the local inhabitants embody the raw power and energy which, in spite of being removed from "delicacy"—indeed, because of it—are inextricably associated with imagination, love, and beauty (cf. 145:2–7).

Nonetheless, in some important ways the poet is still a man apart:

> himself among the others,
> —treads there the same stones
> on which their feet slip as they climb,
> paced by their dogs! . . .
>
> —over-riding
>
> the risks:
>
> pouring down!
> For the flower of a day!

Williams, unlike his friend Pound, does reject the idea that solitude is somehow necessary to the artistic life. As he says in a "Letter to an Australian Editor," the poet "will continue to produce only if his attachments to society continue adequate. If a man in his fatuous dream cuts himself off from that supplying female, he dries up his sources—as Pound did in the end heading straight for literary sterility."[6] As the lines just quoted from *Paterson* suggest, the poet is merely a man, a man among other men with whom he must maintain continuous intercourse if he is even to live. But if he is treading the same stones that the others are treading, his feet, perhaps because of his greater awareness and sensitivity, do not slip as "their feet slip." The "risks" involved in Paterson's climb are considerable. "Pouring down," they threaten to sweep him away to his destruction, and in a sense "ascents" are therefore equivalent to the "descents" from which one must either "come up" or drown.[7]

6. In *Briarcliff Quarterly*, 3 (1946), 208.
7. Cf. 96:1–2 ff.

That the object of the climb is described as a flower is both characteristic and significant. A few lines later Williams refers to the ground as the "passive-possessive" term toward which he, "the positive" term, moves "possessive[ly]" (cf. 57:6). This is not, of course, a movement toward appropriation, but simply the natural movement toward a female principle by a male principle. As we have seen, the "flower" is identical to the "woman" ("A man like a city and a woman like a flower/ —who are in love"), embodying all the meanings we have already seen attached to the female, and Paterson's approach to the flower is simply another way of symbolizing his approach to reality (the Park) through love and imagination. Because of man's mortality, such a relationship is ultimately transient (hence, "the flower *of a day*"), but as the passage which follows emphasizes, such a moment is paradoxically "eternal" as well.

This passage, on first appearance, seems curious even for a poem like *Paterson:*

> The body is tilted slightly forward from the basic standing
> position and the weight thrown on the ball of the foot,
> while the other thigh is lifted and the leg and opposite
> arm are swung forward (fig. 6B). Various muscles, aided   .

It appears to be from some textbook on body mechanics, merely "prose" (albeit rhythmic prose) printed as "poetry." In spite of its queerness, however, I think it can be justified in at least two ways. On the one hand, of course, the kind of arrested motion involved here is another representation of the "moment of the eternal present." On the other hand, as indicated by the continual use of the word "walking," set off typographically for emphasis, the predominant physical activity in Book II that accompanies Paterson's mental observation, analysis, and synthesis, is ambulatory. As a symbol of quest, such movement is of course traditional, and it must never be forgotten that Williams' poem *is* conceived as a Romantic epic in which a quest ("searching the punk-dry rot" for "beauty") is the central action. The quest is a continuous one, however, and can never come to any real conclusion.[8] It is thus a kind of stasis even while it is constantly a motion as well, a state quite vividly conveyed by the static description of movement.

At this point there occurs a fragment of a letter from "C." to "Dr. P.":

> Despite my having said that I'd never write to you again, I do so now because I find, with the passing of time, that the outcome of my failure with you has been the complete damming up of all my creative capacities in a particularly disastrous manner such as I have never before experienced.
>
> For a great many weeks now (whenever I've tried to write poetry) every thought I've had, even every feeling, has been struck off some surface crust of myself which began gathering when I first sensed that you were ignoring the real contents of my last letters to you, and which finally congealed into some impenetrable substance when you asked me to quit corresponding with you altogether without even an explanation.
>
> That kind of blockage, exiling one's self from one's self— have you ever experienced it? I dare say you have, at moments; and if so, you can well understand what a serious psychological injury it amounts to when turned into a permanent day-to-day condition.

The first such fragment occurs near the beginning of Book I (15: 21–16:3), but its implications are not developed. In *Paterson* II,

8. Indeed, this is the very reason why Williams, seven years after the publication of *Paterson* IV had ostensibly "complete[d] his microcosmic, personal, modern epic" (from the news release "News from New Directions," May 31, 1951), surprisingly announced the publication of a *Paterson* V: "I have come to understand not only that many changes have occurred in me and the world, but I have been forced to recognize that there can be no end to such a story I have envisioned with the terms which I had laid down for myself" (dust-jacket comment on 1958 edition of Book V). Even more surprising, perhaps, is the fact that Williams, near the time of his death in 1961, was working on a *Paterson* VI.

however, we get a whole series of them, ultimately constituting almost a fifth of the book's total bulk. In general, these letters are concerned with the breakdown of relationship. The breakdown is itself much the same as the breakdown "among the working classes," but it differs from the latter in being neurotically intellectualized. What the poetess says is easy enough to understand. Her situation is "desperate": her desire to see Dr. P. "not impersonally, but in the most personal of ways" (94:12–13), being thwarted for want of "some little warmth of friendliness and friendship" (93:28–29), has resulted in what she calls the destruction of "the validity for me myself of myself," of her "sense of personal identity" (63:12–14), as well as in the neurotic acedia of which she speaks here. As the excruciating overanalysis, cold intellectualization, and pseudo-literary style of her letters indicate, her "creative capacities" seem decidedly minimal, and her real desire seems simply to drain Dr. P. in order to fill her own abyss. She seems, then, one of the most horrible examples of modern "Puritanism" in the poem. She would appear to be totally appropriative—solipsistically turned in on herself and oblivious to everything save her own "wants" and "needs." As I have tried to show in my discussion of *In the American Grain,* and as I will repeatedly emphasize throughout my discussion of *Paterson,* both life and art depend upon a generous outgoing approach to the world outside oneself. About such emotions the poem's "blocked" poetess seems to know nothing, and her impenetrable surface crust is at last only a symbol of her own self-absorption. All this is not to say that "C." does not need love; on the contrary, she needs it most desperately. But love cannot be had simply for the asking: we receive but what we give.

To the poetess' wordy letters Williams replies with the single line: "How do I love you? These!" The line's source is almost certainly the most famous of Mrs. Browning's *Sonnets from the Portuguese* (XLIII). Tellingly, however, the poet refuses to "count the ways" in which he offers love. He cannot, as the poetess would have him do, offer sympathy and love exclusively to her. Such a "marriage" would be his own undoing, a "marriage only to destroy" (cf. 130:1–5). But he can offer her the inclusive love with which he approaches everything in his world. By loving "These," he somewhat paradoxically loves her as well, and since "These" are uncountable—in their being unappropriated as well as in their being numberless—the ways in which he loves her are infinite.

As Paterson continues to walk through the Park, "He hears . . . Voices indeterminate," among which are the voices of both the Evangelist and the Falls. He watches the people "moving, in groups, by twos and fours — filtering/ off by way of the many bypaths," and listens to their characteristic conversations:

> *I asked him, What do you do?*
>
> *He smiled patiently, The typical American question.*
> *In Europe they would ask, What are you doing? Or,*
> *What are you doing now?*

The first question is indeed "typically American." It means "What do you do for a living?," and immediately characterizes our fundamentally "Puritan" culture. The "European" attitude is somewhat better, for the question "What are you doing now?" ignores almost completely both the past (which is "dead"—cf. 148:8–9) and the future (the concern for which verges on the acquisitive). But even here the odor of "Puritanism" cannot quite be escaped. Further, the European questions tend to betray a little too much interest in "projects"—either artistic ("What are you working on?") or social ("What are you doing for humanity?" or "What are you doing now that things are so bad?"). In any case the ideal questions would be "Upon what are you meditating?" and "What are you creatively imagining?," as the poet implies in the thought which follows:

> *What do I do? I listen, to the water falling.*
> *(No sound of it here but with the wind!) This is my*
> *entire occupation.*

This will be echoed many times, most strikingly when the poet reaffirms his position at the conclusion of *Paterson* III ("The roar,/

the roar of the present . . . is, of necessity, my sole concern"—
172:11–13) and when he turns again "to the water's steady roar,
as of a distant/ waterfall" (237:26–28) at the conclusion of *Paterson* IV. The Falls is constantly associated with imagination, energy,
vital beauty, and the eternal present. To listen to its voice is to
"approach" it, ultimately to become one with it and to "possess" it
without pragmatic design.

There follows a prose account of a rather ugly event occurring in
the Park on a Sunday late in the spring of 1880. The phrase "a
great beast!" (Hamilton's phrase) is inserted in the middle of the
passage as a kind of title:

No fairer day ever dawned anywhere than May 2, 1880,
when the German Singing Societies of Paterson met on Garret
Mountain, as they did many years before on the first Sunday in
May.

However the meeting of 1880 proved a fatal day, when
William Dalzell, who owned a piece of property near the
scene of the festivities, shot John Joseph Van Houten.
Dalzell claimed that the visitors had in previous years walked
over his garden and was determined that this year he would
stop them from crossing any part of his grounds.

Immediately after the shot the quiet group of singers was
turned into an infuriated mob who would take Dalzell into
their own hands. . . . The crowd . . . numbered some ten thousand . . . [Finally] William McNulty, Dean of Saint Joseph's
Catholic Church . . . proceeded to the scene in a hack. Taking
Dalzell by the arm, in full view of the infuriated mob, he
led the man to the hack and seating himself by his side,
ordered the driver to proceed. The crowd hesitated, be-
wildered.

Judgments in an occurrence like this are useless; the point is simply
the basic vulgarity and brutality that lurks largely concealed under
conventional forms and institutions, the horror of a loveless society.

The same "great beast" is in the Park in the twentieth century, but the important question raised by the episode is how such a society is to be "approached." I have already suggested that Williams, like Whitman, sees himself "embracing" such "foulness" (126:19–20). The Dean does not go so far as this, of course, but his actions do imply a considerable degree of sympathy both for Dalzell and for the mob. He presumably condones neither what Dalzell has done nor the mob's furor, and he could vigorously denounce both. But that this would accomplish anything is doubtful, and in any case he would merely be lowering himself to the level of those before him. Thus he says nothing—he does not even judge—and it is this which I think Williams would find most exemplary. As Pound says in a context only slightly different: "If he [Williams] wants to 'do' anything about what he sees, this desire for action does not rise until he has meditated in full and at leisure. Where I want to kill at once, he ruminates."[9]

At this point the prose fragment suddenly breaks off to give way to one of the most magnificent sections in all of *Paterson*, a powerful lyric concerning the process of artistic creation. Paterson is still "Walking" through the Park. "He leaves the path," however, and "finds hard going" in a land of "stubble and matted brambles/ seeming a pasture—but no pasture." Fertility and creativity are alike departed, and only "old furrows" remain "to say labor [presumably both male and female] sweated or/ had sweated here." The "flame" of vitality, passion, and love (cf. 154:18–19) is "spent"; as in the Library of Book III, there remains only "the ruin left/ by the conflagration." In short, Paterson is walking in the exhausted Waste Land of modern "Puritanism."

Suddenly and without warning, there rises out of this desolation a vision of "wonder":

> When! from before his feet, half tripping,
> picking a way, there starts   .
>   a flight of empurpled wings!

9. "Dr. Williams' Position," *Dial*, 85 (1928), 398.

> —invisibly created (their
> jackets dust-grey) from the dust kindled
> to sudden ardor!

These first grasshoppers are almost certainly real. Paterson's movement has stirred them from the undergrowth, where they were unseen and hence invisible. "Invisibly created," however, also suggests another meaning. Not everyone's vision of the flight of ordinary grasshoppers would be like the glorious ("empurpled") vision here, and that the vision here *is* glorious suggests that the poet is indeed "creating" what he "sees." This is not to say that he is necessarily falsifying experience, only that while he is seeing the world through the prosaic eye, he is simultaneously illuminating it ("kindling" it) with the flame of poetic imagination. This is both the process of "half-creation" of which Wordsworth speaks in *Tintern Abbey,* and the "artifice" of which Wallace Stevens speaks in *The Idea of Order at Key West.* An even better description of the process is to be found in the term "invention" as used in traditional rhetoric and poetics, for, as Roy Harvey Pearce has put it, "To invent is at once to find by making and make by finding."[10]

Also introducing the role of the poetic memory, the lyric goes on to emphasize this process of imaginative creation even more:

> They fly away, churring! until
> their strength spent they plunge
> to the coarse cover again and disappear
> —but leave, livening the mind, a flashing
> of wings and a churring song   .

As the first grasshoppers disappear, their energies are "spent" only through the natural course of mortality and decay—not, as in

10. *American Poetry,* p. 112. In a speech before the members of the English Institute in 1948, Williams said, "until your artists have conceived you [man and his world] in your unique and supreme form you can never conceive yourselves and have not, in fact, existed."

the case of the "Puritan" inhabitants of the Waste Land, through any willful negation. Appropriately, then, they beget new images in the mind, images indistinguishable from their "precedents." From this point on, in fact, we can never be quite sure whether the poet is speaking of grasshoppers that are real or grasshoppers that are imagined. But it does not matter. The whole point is that the real and the imagined become identical.

As reality, imagination, and memory coalesce into one, there emerges what Williams calls "a grasshopper of red basalt":

> AND a grasshopper of red basalt, boot-long,
> tumbles from the core of his mind . . .
> —boot long
> window-eyes that front the whole head,
>   Red stone! as if
> a light still clung in them   .

Besides being the memory of an actual carving from Chapultepec, this stone grasshopper is, in one sense, an "idea" of a work of art, though deriving from the apprehended world and not independent of it. In another sense it is simply the "image" of the yet-to-be-created work as it exists in the mind. But the image or idea is conceived so much as a "thing" (the poet even speaks of its "weight"), that the stone grasshopper ultimately "exists" as the tangible work of art as well, a record of the creative process which simultaneously embodies the process itself. The wings of the stone grasshopper

>   . . . do not unfold for flight—
> no need!
> the weight (to the hand) finding
> a counter-weight or counter buoyancy
> by the mind's wings   .

Its power and suggestiveness are further indicated by the lines, "a rubble-bank disintegrating beneath a/ tropic downpour," and by the exclamations "Chapultepec! grasshopper hill!" The lines

—a matt stone solicitously instructed
to bear away some rumor
of the living presence that has preceded
it, out-precedented its breath .

thus apply not only to the previous presence of the living grasshoppers but even to the rather remote memories connected with this
presence. In both cases the past is being brought over into the
present.

The lyric rises to a climax:

He is afraid! What then?

Before his feet, at each step, the flight
is renewed. A burst of wings, a quick
churring sound :

   couriers to the ceremonial of love!

—aflame in flight!
  —aflame only in flight!

     No flesh but the caress!

He is led forward by their announcing wings.

The continually renewed flights of the grasshoppers, the continually
repeated bursts of color, flame, and motion rising and falling around
the protagonist as he walks, have gradually become identified with
the Falls of the Passaic itself. To quote a passage in Book III which is
remarkably similar to both the passage in Book II we are considering
and the description of the Falls in Book I, the Falls

  tumbles and rights itself
  and refalls—and does not cease, falling
  and refalling with a roar, a reverberation
  not of the falls but of its rumor
      unabated. [119:5–9]

57

"Falling and refalling" in an eternal present, the Falls does indeed create what Louis Martz has aptly called "a quivering and terrifying scene of beauty."[11] The association of the flying grasshoppers with the Falls is strengthened by the emphasis on sound ("churring," "roaring") and by the use of such words as "plunge," "tumble," "counter-buoyancy," "downpour," and even "falls."

The reference to "announcing wings" marks this moment as being central to the poem. It is the moment, in fact, in which the poetic quest is given an almost divine sanction. On one level the announcing wings are the wings of imagination, the wings "aflame in flight! / —aflame only in flight!" They are also, however, the wings of Cupids, "couriers to the ceremonial of love"; for in the process of kindling the dust to sudden ardor, love and imagination are virtually one and the same. The coming of love, then, is being announced as well as the coming of imagination, and the poet is ultimately associated with Christ, as well as with Eros, Pegasus, and perhaps even Apollo.

Immediately following this triumphant affirmation of love and poetry, and before the concluding section of the lyric, there is inserted a fragment from another of the poetess' letters. Its functions are somewhat complex, for besides merely reminding us of her lovelessness and imaginative sterility, it tends subtly to undercut what the poet has celebrated just before. He *has* failed to respond to "C.," even though he is presumably quite capable of doing so. She will later write:

You might as well take all your own literature and everyone else's and toss it into one of those big garbage trucks of the Sanitation Department, so long as the people with the top-cream minds and the "finer" sensibilities use those minds and sensibilities not to make themselves more humane human beings than the average person, but merely as means of ducking responsibility toward a better understanding of their fellow

11. "Recent Poetry," *Yale Review,* 38 (1948), 149.

men, except theoretically—which doesn't mean a God damned
thing.   [101:10–20]

Perhaps in the very printing of these letters Paterson (or Williams?)
does admit to a certain failure here, but as I have suggested, he
cannot accede to her demands for an exclusive, "Puritan" love without utterly destroying himself.

The lyric now concludes, reaffirming the power of a more inclusive love to foster the eternities of imagination and art:

>   —his mind a red stone carved to be
> endless flight   .
> Love that is a stone endlessly in flight,
> so long as stone shall last bearing
> the chisel's stroke   .
>
>
>   .   .   and is lost and covered
> with ash, falls from an undermined bank
> and — begins churring!
> AND DOES, the stone after the life!
>
> The stone lives, the flesh dies
> —we know nothing of death. . . .
>
> Love
>
>   combating sleep
>   _____
>
>   the sleep
>   piecemeal

"The stone" symbolizes the "eternity," at least "so long as stone
shall last" or in the "eternal moment," of the worlds of both imagination and art. In *Paterson* V, too, statements that "the world/ of the
imagination most endures" (248:28–29) and that "A WORLD OF
ART . . . THROUGH THE YEARS HAS/*SURVIVED!*" (244:1–3)
are associated with stone and rock. Love, which brings these worlds

into being (kindling the dust to sudden ardor, giving flight to stone, perceiving glory in an ordinary, even ugly, reality), is also eternal, and it is thus a further meaning associated with "the stone." Though the flesh dies, man himself can also partake of these eternities, for when he is in harmony with them—when he is loving, imagining, and creating, becoming one with these eternities as he becomes one with the Falls—he will "know nothing of death." The passage ends with a final affirmation of the power of love to combat the death-in-life of a fragmented, "Puritan" existence. As the poet will write in the great hymn to love in Book III, "what is there but love, that stares death/ in the eye, love, begetting marriage—/ not infamy, not death" (130:11–13).

To some extent, the prose passage which follows offers "relief" from the intense poetry surrounding it (it ends with the word "fun"), but the fact that it occurs in a serious context seems to suggest that it should also be read in terms of the general theme:

> Shortly after midnight, August 20, 1878, special officer Goodridge, when, in front of the Franklin House, heard a strange squealing noise down towards Ellison Street. Running to see what was the matter, he found a cat at bay under the water table at Clark's hardward store on the corner, confronting a strange black animal too small to be a cat and entirely too large for a rat. . . . Mr. Goodridge made several strikes at it with his club but was unable to hit it. Then officer Keyes came along and as soon as he saw it, he said it was a mink, which confirmed the theory that Mr. Goodridge had already formed. Both tried for a while to hit it with their clubs but were unable to do so, when finally officer Goodridge drew his pistol and fired a shot at the animal. The shot evidently missed its mark, but the noise and powder so frightened the little joker that it jumped out into the street, and made down into Ellison Street at a wonderful gait, closely followed by the two officers.

Like the grasshoppers, the mink appears suddenly and without warning, and it too seems to be a natural "wonder." But while the officers have their "fun" with it, their actions are nonetheless brutal and appropriative. Unlike the poet of the previous lyric, they are incapable of "approach," and their intentions are ultimately destructive. Like the grasshoppers which "plunge/ to the coarse cover again and disappear," the "mink disappear[s] down a cellar window under the grocery store below Spangermacher's lager beer saloon." But unlike the grasshoppers which leave behind, for the sensitive poet, both a memory and an enlivened creative imagination, the mink leaves, for the "Puritan" officers, nothing: "that was the last seen of it. The cellar was examined again in the morning, but nothing further could be *discovered* of the little critter that had caused so much fun" (italics mine).

Thus the poet may once more reaffirm the position of the "grasshopper" lyric, repeating his basic point in a passage which reads almost like an oracle:[12]

> Without invention nothing is well spaced,
> unless the mind change, unless
> the stars are new measured, according
> to their relative positions, the
> line will not change, the necessity
> will not matriculate: unless there is
> a new mind there cannot be a new
> line, the old will go on
> repeating itself with recurring
> deadliness: without invention
> nothing lies under the witch-hazel
> bush, the alder does not grow from among
> the hummocks . . .
> . . . without invention the line
> will never again take on its ancient
> divisions when the word, a supple word,
> lived in it, crumbled now to chalk.

12. Cf. *Deep Religious Faith,* in *PB* 95–96.

Louis Martz has suggested that this passage, particularly in its use of the repeated phrase "without invention," "seems to echo wryly one of the most famous passages of Pound, Canto 45, on usury, where Pound adopts the manner of a medieval or a renaissance preacher." Williams, Martz goes on to say, insists "that bold exploration of the local will result in the discovery of a new world blossoming about him. Pound's mind lives at its best among the splendors of ancient human artifacts and when these splendors seem threatened, Pound seeks a social answer."[13] Williams, then, is here subtly protesting against any vision of existence, like that of Pound's *Cantos,* for example, which is fundamentally pessimistic with respect to the present. An especially relevant comment in the *Autobiography* has become somewhat notorious, but it is so often quoted out of context, it is worth looking at in its entirety. The poet is writing of the early 1920s:

> These were the years just before the great catastrophe to our letters—the appearance of T. S. Eliot's *The Waste Land.* There was heat in us, a core and a drive that was gathering headway upon the theme of a rediscovery of a primary impetus, the elementary principle of all art, in the local conditions. Our work staggered to a halt for a moment under the blast of Eliot's genius . . . We did not know how to answer him.   [146][14]

In *Paterson,* of course, Williams does know how to answer Eliot, and, in his Whitmanesque affirmation of the local, he has made truly possible a rediscovery of the primary impetus of both life and art. Only invention—i.e. loving imagination—can bring ultimate order and unity out of the vast chaos of the apprehended universe.[15] And unless the mind change, relating itself to the present and approaching the world outside as this world exists in the here and now, the "line"—both the poetic line, the final record of human imagination

13. "The Unicorn in *Paterson,*" pp. 548–49.
14. Cf. *P* 10:2–3.
15. Cf. the "Blessed rage for order" in Stevens' *Key West.*

62

and creativity, and the line of the race's development—will stagnate even more than it already has. It will repeat itself, not with the positive recurrence associated with the Falls or with the flights of the grasshoppers, but with a cycle that becomes more confining each time around.[16]

What Paterson/Williams has preached (literally, as Martz' comments imply) he now puts into practice. He begins by composing an extraordinary lyric on a pair of young lovers sunning in the Park. It is 11 o'clock, *before* the ascent to the cliff, which takes place in the afternoon, perhaps implying that what is accomplished in this lyric is a kind of preparation for what is accomplished in the earlier one. The two lovers lie "Under the bush," "protected/ from the offending sun." They appear as if they are talking, but the poet says that in reality they only "seem to talk," because their language is inadequate.[17] Yet in another sense they *are* talking, through a "love" which although decayed is "beyond all talk." To be sure, this love is almost grossly sensual:

> beneath
>
> the sun in frank vulgarity. . . .
>
> . . . Semi-roused
>
> they lie upon their blanket
> face to face

But if they are "flagrant," like the "3 colored girls" who pass by, they are "Not undignified" (the tone imparted by the meiosis is significant). Nor are they entirely "divorced": they do lie "face to face," they "do meet/ in the flesh" (and this is not "half-hearted, spasmodic coupling—signs of the failure of love").[18] The phrase

16. Like the Orc Cycle described by Blake in *The Mental Traveller* and in the prophetic works.
17. Cf. 24:32–25:2 and esp. 20:23–21:11.
18. Pearce, *American Poetry*, p. 121.

"in perfect domesticity" is therefore only partly ironic. If "SOME sort/ of breakdown/ has occurred," something of a previously vital wholeness has also remained.

That this is so Williams suggests by emphasizing, particularly toward the end of the lyric, a mythic or archetypal pattern which lies just beneath the "modern replica":

> And having *bathed*
>
> and having *eaten* (a few
> sandwiches)
> their pitiful thoughts *do meet*
>
> *in the flesh*—surrounded
> by churring loves! Gay wings
> to bear them (in sleep)
>
> —their thoughts alight,
> away
> .   .   among the grass.   [italics mine]

This is a device Williams might well have learned, ironically enough, from *The Waste Land.* But whereas Eliot stresses the degeneration of mythic archetypes, Williams stresses the extent to which they are still alive. The Cupids that surround the lovers ("Churring loves"—cf. grasshopper lyric) suggest that love, at least in some form, remains. Even some slight imaginative activity seems to be suggested by the "Gay wings" that "bear . . . their thoughts away" to "alight . . . among the grass."

If love is the subject of this lyric, love is also its source. Without the sensibility which sees even the "flagrant," "vagrant" world of the Park as "approachable," it would be impossible. But as Williams puts it in a kind of title to the passage, to the loving, imaginative man "a park . . . devoted to pleasure" is also a park "devoted to   . grasshoppers!" Williams' love, indeed, is the supreme triumph of the poem:

I was impassioned when I wrote Part II [of Paterson]. I had just been out on the mountain. I was always concerned with the plight of the young in the industrial age who are affected by love. . . . I love the impassioned simplicity of young lovers. When it's thwarted, and they don't know it's thwarted, then the vulgarity is lifted to distinction by being treated with the very greatest in art which I can conceive.

It's easy to miss, but the whole theme of *Paterson* is brought out in this passage [*P* 66–67], the contrast between the mythic beauty of the Falls and Mountain and the industrial hideousness. But they haven't been able to lick us. To escape as an artist, to escape from the scene would be a defeat for me. But I will not be licked; so in this scene love has triumphed. If I as artist had separated myself from the scene, it would be a defeat. But I have not. I have made myself a part of the scene.[19]

As I have shown, another man who made himself a part of the local scene was Père Sebastian Rasles. This may well provide the key to the curious passage which comes next. "Walking—/ across the old swale," which is "marked still by the line of Indian alders," Paterson thinks back on the Indian raids of the past:

> .   .   they (the Indians) would weave
> in and out, unseen, among them along the stream
>
> .   come out whooping between the log
> house and men working the field, cut them
> off! they having left their arms in the block-
> house, and—without defense—carry them away
> into captivity. One old man   .

19. Conversation with John C. Thirlwall, Apr. 8, 1954. In John C. Thirlwall, "William Carlos Williams' *Paterson:* The Search for The Redeeming Language—A Personal Epic in Five Parts," *New Directions* 17 (1961), 276–77.

To be sure, this may be viewed as merely another example of brutality and the failure of love. But the real meaning of these lines seems to lie elsewhere. In *In the American Grain* this important passage occurs just after Williams has described Rasles as having "lived with his village—alone, absorbed in them":

> For his [Rasles'] presentation of the Indian point of view toward the raids on the English settlements alone, his letters are invaluable. If the Puritans feared the savage—his admirable enthusiasm for their high merit as warriors is very beautiful. "The way they make war, these people, renders a handful of their warriors more redoubtable than would be a corps of two or three thousand European soldiers." . . . It is an enthusiasm that possesses him.   [121–22]

The significance of the passage in *Paterson,* then, lies not so much in the Indians' attitude toward the white men as in the poet's attitude toward the Indians, in his "enthusiastic" affirmation of their native vigor and beauty. Such an attitude is ultimately related to the poet's attitude of reconciliation and "approach" to far less justifiable brutality in the present.

But references to the past such as these are unconventional and not easily grasped by the reader. *In the American Grain* fell flat when it was first published, and even today "its place among the primary works of American literature" is not quite so "widely recognized" as the blurb on the back cover of the 1956 paperback would have us believe. Pound's comment—"The lack of celerity in his process, the unfamiliarity with facile or with established solutions would account for the irritation his earlier prose [he cites *In the American Grain*], as I remember it, caused to sophisticated Britons. 'How any man could go on talking about such things!' and so on"[20]—would apply equally well on this side of the Atlantic. In *Paterson,* I think, Williams is attempting to rewrite *In the*

20. "Dr. Williams' Position," p. 398.

American Grain in a different, more accessible, mode. The past is still important, but he is now writing primarily in terms of the present. His comment, after interrupting the story of "One old man" before he has even begun it, seems to suggest this:

> Forget it! for God's sake, Cut
> out that stuff   .

At this point, therefore, he "rejoins the path" in more ways than one (cf. 61:23). As he does so, he "sees, on a treeless/ knoll—the red path choking it—/ a stone wall, a sort of circular/ redoubt against the sky, barren and/ unoccupied." This appears to be another Waste Land, a repetition on another level of the Waste Land out of which the grasshoppers arise. It is also associated with the "chronic hills" that lie "to the north." Paterson decides to "Mount," and at once realizes another vision of the dependency of art and life upon love:

> He stops short:
> Who's here?

> To a stone bench, to which she's leashed, within the wall a man in tweeds—a pipe hooked in his jaw—is combing out a new-washed Collie bitch. The deliberate comb-strokes part the long hair—even her face he combs though her legs tremble slightly—until it lies, as he designs, like ripples in white sand giving off its clean-dog odor. The floor, stone slabs, she stands patiently before his caresses in that bare "sea chamber."

We may recall the image of "combing" from the beginning of Book I (15:12–15). For the poet this unraveling and separating of the various strands of experience one from the other is an act of love, a "caress" (tellingly, both "the Collie" and "the world" are "she's"), an attempt to "approach" the things of his world "concretely." It is the dispersal into particulars which must precede a transfiguring

67

metamorphosis. In the passage from Book II this "caress" is literally identified with the transfiguration, for not only is order "invented" out of disorder, but that order itself is associated with "newness" and "cleanness" (cf. the "bathing" associated with the two lovers). It should especially be noted that although this order is "deliberately" imposed, it is also "natural"; for if the man is combing the long hair until it lies as he "designs," he is, in the end, only allowing its natural form to manifest itself. This is supported by the fact that the dog is leashed to a bench made of "stone"—symbol of both the "grounding" of love, imagination, and art in "reality" and the natural eternity in which these exist.

The phrase with which this passage ends—"sea chamber" (in quotation marks)—suggests that Williams is here subtly and deliberately parodying *The Love Song of J. Alfred Prufrock*. The "man in tweeds" is therefore a positive answer to Eliot's negative description of modern man. Eliot's poem concludes as follows:

> I have seen them riding seaward on the waves
> Combing the white hair of the waves blown back
> When the wind blows the water white and black.
>
> We have lingered in the chambers of the sea
> By sea-girls wreathed with seaweed red and brown
> Till human voices wake us, and we drown.

Unlike Paterson/Williams, who is active, Prufrock is purely passive. It is the mermaids who are riding on the waves; Prufrock only stands watching them from the beach. The mermaids, associated with vitality and beauty, are "Combing the white hair of the waves," but Prufrock cannot even decide how he should part his own hair (note the many parallel wordings in these two poems—"combing," "part," "hair," "white"—as well as the similar uses of beach sand and ripples). While Prufrock "drowns" or suffers the death-in-life of being "a pair of ragged claws/ Scuttling across the floors of silent seas," Paterson/Williams lives. He stands on a "floor" of "stone slabs" which, like the stone grasshoppers, symbolize his "grounding" in "eternity."

Against this affirmation of love and imagination, Williams sets an amusing letter about an "awful event" that has happened to another female dog:

> Dear B. Please excuse me for not having told you this when I was over to your house. I had no courage to answer your questions so I'll write it. Your dog *is* going to have puppies although I prayed she would be okey. It wasn't that she was left alone as she never was but I used to let her out at dinner time while I hung up my clothes. . . . *Every few* seconds I would run to the end of the line or peek under the sheets to see if Musty was alright. She was until I looked a minute too late.

The writer of this letter is clearly a "Puritan." She "prays" that natural impulses be constrained even among animals. Like the poetess, she would "block" creative vitality, and like officers Goodridge and Keyes, she would, as it were, frighten a wonder away: "I took sticks and stones after the dog but he wouldn't beat it. . . . I started praying that I had frightened the other dog so much that nothing had happened." Both to her and to her correspondent, Musty (the name contrasts wittily to the "clean-dog odor" of the Collie) is only a pet—an animal appropriated for use by its owner ("Your dog"). The comic treatment of this episode, of course, implies a more or less reconciled (inclusive) attitude to it on the part of the poet.

It is "now early afternoon," and "still the picnickers come on . . . and scatter through the/ trees over the fenced-in acres":

> Loiterers in groups straggle
> over the bare rock-table—scratched by their
> boot-nails more than the glacier scratched
> them—walking indifferent through
> each other's privacy   .

In Book III the poet will call this indifference the "indifference of certain death" (129:9–10). On another level, however, the "stroking" is also the caressing/combing involved in the Collie episode, and the "pleasure" it provides is the pleasure of imaginative metamorphosis. Near the end of the section, in fact, we learn that even the feet of the picnickers have pradoxically "polished" the rocks.

The problem, then, is "approach." Prufrock, capable of salvation only in "dreams," hears human voices and drowns. But if Paterson approaches with love and imagination the voices that he hears—

> Voices!
> multiple and inarticulate . voices
> clattering loudly to the sun, to
> the clouds. Voices!
> assaulting the air gaily from all sides

—if he thus approaches these voices, he will find salvation in the here and now. This is precisely what the Evangelist who appears in Section II will "preach," and it is for his reassuring voice that Paterson now seeks:

> —among which the ear strains to catch
> the movement of one voice among the rest
> —a reed-like voice
>> of peculiar accent...

> —his voice, one among many (unheard)
> moving under all.[21]

As yet only "a trumpet sounds fitfully" (cf. 80:5), but even this is a sufficient intimation of the voice's presence:

21. Possibly these lines could also be read in terms of the poet's trying to separate individual voices from one another, combing out the speech, or on another level, in terms of his trying to hear the Evangelist's voice *within* these other voices. But these interpretations are only secondary.

> —and the imagination soars, as a voice
> beckons, a thundrous voice, endless
> —as sleep: the voice
> that has ineluctably called them—
> > that unmoving roar!
> churches and factories
> > (at a price)
> together, summoned them from the pit   .

The Evangelist's voice has summoned churches and factories from the abyss of loveless "Puritanism," preaching the gospel of love at enormous cost to himself (the cost motif becomes especially important later). "The imagination soars" toward the beckoning voice exactly as it soars when beholding a hawk (71:6–7) or a woman's face (41:19–42:21). It is, in fact, to the imaginative apprehension of just such things that the Evangelist's words may lead. Even here the Evangelist is associated with the Falls: "the *movement* of one voice," "a *thundrous* voice, *endless* . . . that *unmoving* roar," "his voice . . . unheard" paralleling the plunging Falls "unseen."

Paterson now moves toward "the idlers' favorite/ haunts, the picturesque summit." As he walks his voice mingles with other voices

> —the voice in his voice
> opening his old throat, blowing out his lips,
> kindling his mind (more
> than his mind will kindle).

One may recall the previous image of kindling—namely, the kindling of the dust to sudden ardor in the grasshopper lyric. As there the world is kindled by the loving, imaginative mind, so here the mind is itself kindled by the voice of love. This voice is the underlying principle within the protagonist; as it widens his consciousness, it opens his throat to sing of love and imagination.

Once at the summit, "the center of movement, the core of gaiety," Paterson observes another group of picnickers:

> Here a young man, perhaps sixteen,
> is sitting with his back to the rock among
> some ferns playing a guitar, dead pan   .
>
> The rest are eating and drinking.
>
>   The big guy
> in the black hat is too full to move   .

As in the earlier scene of the two lovers, there are some ritual over-
tones here in the music, eating, and drinking, but the main function
of these lines is simply to convey the "indifference" and deathlike
"sleep" of the "masses." The tone here is not so elevated as the tone
of either the earlier episode or the passage which follows:

>   but Mary
> is up!
>   Come on! Wassa ma'? You got
> broken leg? . . .
>
>   —lifts one arm holding the cymbals
> of her thoughts, cocks her old head
> and dances! raising her skirts:
>
>   La la la la!
>
> What a bunch of bums! Afraid somebody see
> you!
>   Blah!
>   *Excrementi!*
>   —she spits.
> Look a' me, Grandma! Everybody too damn
> lazy.

The exuberance and vitality here are again, perhaps, vulgar. But as
we shall see, "Vulgarity surpasses all perfections . . . surmounting

the world, its core" (145:5–10), and in addition, it is dignified by being identified with the oldest of mythic rituals:

> This is the old, the very old, old upon old,
> the undying: even to the minute gestures,
> the hand holding the cup, the wine
> spilling, the arm stained by it.

Mary is re-enacting a kind of Bacchanalian revel, complete with the dancing, music, and "tipsy excess" described by Frazer,[22] though these are all in a somewhat debased form. What is important, however, is that the vital rituals have been brought over from the past into the present ("and the old cultures intoxicates [sic] them:/ present!")—made "undying" by being perpetually revitalized by the imaginations of those who are not "too damn/ lazy."

At this point Williams inserts a passage which almost certainly refers to a scene in Sergei Eisenstein's "lost" film, *Que Viva Mexico!*[23] Eisenstein's depiction of the robustness and spontaneity of the "Mexican cowboy," as well as his closeness to the "ground," would have been especially interesting to Williams:

22. Sir James George Frazer, *The New Golden Bough,* ed. Theodor H. Gaster (New York, New American Library, 1964), p. 417.

23. For information regarding this film see Sergei Eisenstein, *"Film Form" and "The Film Sense,"* ed. and trans. Jay Leyda (Cleveland, World Publishing Co., Meridian Books, 1957), pp. 225, 251–55, 272–73. The film was begun in the early 1930s, and Eisenstein even went to Mexico to begin production, but as a result of various immorality charges, he was recalled to Russia before it was completed. The footage actually shot for the film was apparently confiscated and used by various others in the films *Thunder Over Mexico, Death Day,* and *Time in the Sun.* My quotation comes from Eisenstein's incomplete outline of the film which occurs on pp. 251–55. The following statements from this draft are also of interest in regard to *Paterson:* "The man of Yucatan today. The same man who lived thousands of years ago. Unmovable. Unchanging. Eternal. And the great wisdom of Mexico about death. The unity of death and life. The passing of one and the birth of the next one. The eternal circle. . . . Catholicism and paganism. The Virgin of Guadalupe worshipped by wild dances and bloody bull-fights."

  Remember

    the peon in the lost
    Eisenstein film drinking

    from a wine-skin with the abandon
    of a horse drinking

    so that it slopped down his chin?
    down his neck, dribbling

    over his shirt-front and down
    onto his pants—laughing, toothless?

                              Heavenly man!

On one level at least, this last line tends almost to apotheosize the
human, and it might even suggest a reference to Christ. Throughout
the sequence, in fact, Williams seems to be deliberately introducing
Christian elements—notably, the Virgin Mary, Christ, and the Communion ritual—in order to place them within a context of radical
and overt paganism. The pagan "approach" is vulgar, of course, but
at least it is an approach. To the "Puritan" sensibility, this is all
intolerable:

                         Rejected. Even the film
    suppressed   :   but   .   persistent.

Such a sensibility is totally incapable of seeing how "fertility" and
"drunkenness" (cf. 16:20–21) might be associated with "cleansed"
purity (cf. 245:14). But such meanings are understandable as well
as persistent to individuals like "Mary," Eisenstein's peon, and the
poet.

    The episode which now occurs is both a parallel and a contrast
to the episode which occurs just before. Still walking among "The

picnickers laugh[ing] on the rocks celebrating/ the varied Sunday
of their loves with/ its declining light," Paterson looks down from
a ledge into a "grassy den/ (somewhat removed from the traffic)" in
which there are two lovers. Like the pair of lovers he sees earlier in
the section, who lie "beneath/ the sun in frank vulgarity," the lovers
here "lie/ overt upon the grass":

> She stirs, distraught,
> against him—wounded (drunk), moves
> against him (a lump) desiring,
> against him, bored   .
>
> flagrantly bored and sleeping, a
> beer bottle still grasped spear-like
> in his hand . . .
>
>   —moving nearer
> she—lean as a goat—leans
> her lean belly to the man's backside
> toying with the clips of his
> suspenders   .

As in the scene just before, it is only the female who is in the least
active. But she is hardly another Mary. Both women are presumably
drunk, but where this one only "stirs," Mary "dances." Yet even here
the breakdown of love is not altogether complete; for just as the
earliest couple is surrounded by Cupids in the form of "churring
loves," so this one is surrounded by Cupids in the form of "the small,
sleepless boys, who/ have climbed the columnar rocks." To be sure,
these Cupids are "puzzled" and "bored equally," but it is emphasized
that this is only because they watch "in the sexless/ light (of childhood)." If they "go charging off" again, this may be simply because
they do not know that their presence is required.

As Section I draws to a close, the voice of the Evangelist becomes
more and more important: "the movement throbs openly/ and you

can hear the Evangelist shouting!" To this shouting, Paterson adds his own "useless voice"—useless in two senses. Like the Evangelist's, his voice proclaims the gospel of "use-less," unappropriative love, and like the Evangelist's, it seems to accomplish nothing:

> until there moves in his sleep
> a music that is whole, unequivocal in
> his sleep, sweating in his sleep—laboring
> against sleep, agasp!)
> 　　　　　　　　—and does not waken.

> Sees, alive (asleep)
> 　　　　—the fall's roar entering
> in his sleep—scattered over the mountain
> severally　　.

> 　　　—by which he woos her, severally.

The two voices harmonize, and the music of an unambiguous whole-ness moves within both Paterson the man and Paterson the city-giant. The giant, as we read in Book I, is of course "Eternally asleep" (14:4), but this "sleep" must not be confused with the sleep of death-in-life against which Paterson the man, like all imaginative men, labors. The "music" finally becomes the roar of the Falls, em-bodying not only the voice of the Evangelist but also love, beauty, art, and the eternal present. As the Falls' roar rolls through both man and giant, each is revitalized, and since the giant is the animating force of the world of Paterson, this new vitality will come also to inform the scattered Patersonians wandering in the Park (the phrase "to be fulfilled" recalls the "annunciation" at the climax of the grasshopper lyric). These people, like the protagonist, would then be able to woo the mountain—i.e. the "world"—successfully.

But if such a power is available to it, the "amnesic crowd" is unmoved. It is cut off from its sources of power and life as it is cut off from its origins. If Paterson "strains to catch the movement" of the "one voice" of the Evangelist (70:11–14), the crowd "strains/ to catch the movement" only of the "one voice" of "Pleasure." This it "hears"; but it is "relived," not "reborn," caught in the cycle of "recurring deadliness" (65:16–17).

The actual ending of Section I, with the reference to "A cop . . . directing traffic/ across the main road up/ a little wooded slope toward/ the conveniences," is difficult. The traffic straining up this slope contrasts markedly with the solitary poet climbing to the visions of the grasshoppers, the Collie, and the various lovers. But as the verse witnesses, even this vision of the great beast is ultimately approached by the poet with some degree of sympathy and imagination. Thus the final lines:

> deformity—
>
> —to be deciphered (a horn, a trumpet!)
> an elucidation by multiplicity,
> a corrosion, a parasitic curd, a clarion
> for belief, to be good dogs   :
>
> NO DOGS ALLOWED AT LARGE IN THIS PARK.

Like all "true wit," these lines are ultimately serious. The modern world's vulgarity ("corrosion," "parasitism," "curdling"—cf. 66: 22–67:3) must be "deciphered"; from its nothingness and meaninglessness the poet must create and discover—that is, "invent"—meaning. The key to such a process is to be learned from the Evangelist, whose voice, like the sound of his band, is a clarion for belief in love. Such love will free man from the ("Puritan") bonds by which he is constrained, enabling him once again to approach his world "at large." Love in no form will be viewed as "bad": even Musty will be seen as an emblem of "good." As we have already seen, love necessarily involves "dispersal"—leading to "multiplicity." But after such an "elucidation" of the thing's individuality, there may follow a re-unifying, imaginative "metamorphosis"—"By multiplication a reduction to one."

THE VOICE OF THE EVANGELIST

Section II begins with the single word "Blocked," a word which is taken from one of the poetess' letters (59:28) and which sums up her situation precisely. Her situation is hardly unique, however, and in the end it is symptomatic of most of her world.[24] At this point, then, the sardonic voice which mocks the poet throughout the poem bitterly suggests that he sing only of the breakdown:

> Blocked.
>   (Make a song out of that: concretely)

Ironically, of course, Williams does make a song out of the unloving, unimaginative world around him—the song of his "reconciliation" and "concrete approach" to it. But it is more important to see that in the remainder of Section II he ignores the challenging voice and instead makes a song out of yet another example of the love that has survived—indeed, out of the best example he can find, the love proclaimed by the Evangelist.

Before actually dealing with the Evangelist, however, the poet reiterates, in a rather polemical manner, the basic sources of ("By whom" is fostered) the "blockage" which the Evangelist would overcome. The first source he cites is the conventional, "Puritan" church:[25]

> In its midst rose a massive church.   .   .   And it all
> came to me then—that those poor souls had nothing else in the
> world, save that church, between them and the eternal stony,
> ungrateful and unpromising dirt they lived by . . . . .

Such a church offers a Heaven, but a Heaven only in the future. How love and imagination can transform the apparent waste land of

24. Cf. 46:23–27.
25. It should be obvious that the church involved here is not of any particular denomination.

the present, however, we have already seen in the grasshopper lyric. Moreover, such a church perpetuates itself by claiming to "save" man from the physical and spiritual "dirtiness" which he is and from the "dirt" which he is ultimately to become. But in turning man away from the people and things of his world, it is in reality separating him from the "ground" which is his only hope (the ground, ironically, really *is* "eternal"—or "stony"; it is anything but "ungrateful" and "unpromising"). Just as the church, in "restricting" the "knowledge" of a Rasles or a Williams, is greatly responsible for the "orchestral dullness" which overlays man's world, so, in "raising" man above the ground, it prevents the "descent" which is so central to Williams' position.

The second source of "blockage" that the poet mentions at this point is "society" or "government":

> I see they—the Senate, is trying to block Lilienthal and deliver "the bomb" over to a few industrialists. I don't think they will succeed but   .   .   that is what I mean when I refuse to get excited over the cry, Communist! they use to blind us. It's terrifying to think how easily we can be destroyed, a few votes. Even though Communism is a threat, are Communists any *worse* than the guilty bastards trying in that way to undermine us?

As usual, Williams is reading American history in terms of his myth. In the historical episode to which this quotation refers, he sees an attempt on the part of organized society to give supreme power to, virtually to deify, the highest representatives of appropriative, use-oriented pragmatism. That such an action could even be conceived, let alone begun, witnesses for him the pervasiveness of the "Puritan" attitude toward life.

Faitoute, who has been "standing with his back/ to the lions' pit/ (where the drunken lovers [sleep], now, both of them)/ indifferent," now starts "again wandering—foot pacing foot outward/ into emptiness." Having failed to find a great deal of love in his world, he acknowledges that he is "sick of his diversions." But he is still "proud of women"; he still has faith that the female principle of love, imagination, and beauty will "requite" him for his uninterrupted quest. As if to confirm this faith, the presence of the Evangelist is announced by the unexpected sound of his band. "Music blurts out" as "suddenly" as the grasshoppers rise from the dust in Section I, and as in the earlier sequence, the sudden apprehension of beauty is the prelude to a vision of love. The scene is described in detail:

> a
> cramped arena has been left clear at the base
> of the observation tower near the urinals. This
> is the Lord's line: Several broken benches
> drawn up in a curving row against the shrubbery
> face the flat ground, benches on which
> a few children have been propped by the others
> against their running off   .
> Three middle aged men with iron smiles
> stand behind the benches—backing (watching)
> the kids, the kids and several women—and
> holding,
>   a cornet, clarinet and trombone,
> severally, in their hands, at rest.
>   There is also,
> played by a woman, a portable organ   .   .

It is not, of course, with these people that Williams is really concerned. They are, in fact, depicted as automatons, mechanically "forcing out" (85:1) appropriate supporting gestures when the Evangelist requires them and providing a diversion when the Evangelist himself is not speaking. Their "iron smiles" betray their "orchestral dullness," and we may assume that they are almost as indifferent to the Evangelist's message as are their children, who are present only because they are forced to be (they sing only "when prodded"). The "iron smiles" seem peculiarly Blakean, iron being continually associated in Blake with "Urizenic" repression and re-straint. They relate the Evangelist's assistants to the "massive church."

The most interesting phrase in this description is "the Lord's line." It comes directly after the second reference to the line of picnickers streaming up the slope "toward the conveniences," and the humor-ous, even ironic, juxtaposition is surely deliberate. But "the Lord's line" is not only the line of "Christian Soldiers" behind the Evan-gelist; it is also the "line" he is "handing" them—a line which, being "traditional," is dangerously close to being a string of hollow clichés. Such a line, however, is not necessarily stale, and it is indeed endowed with a certain vitality by the Evangelist's enthusiasm. It is, then, neither the conventional line of the "churches," nor the repressive and loveless line in which the "supple word" has "crumbled now to chalk," but rather the newly "invented" line, found as well as made, of love and charity. It might also be noticed that "the Lord's line," finally, seems to refer to the whole of *Paterson*—Williams' new line, his song of love. While Williams has broadened traditional ideas of Christian love considerably, *Paterson* is a sermon that celebrates such love throughout.

The Evangelist himself is described as a kind of cross between a Hebrew prophet and St. Francis of Assisi:[26]

> Before them an old man,
> wearing a fringe of long white hair, bareheaded,
> his glabrous skull reflecting the sun's
> light and in shirtsleeves, is beginning to
> speak—
>
> calling to the birds and trees!
>
> Jumping up and down in his ecstasy he beams
> into the empty blue, eastward, over the parapet
> toward the city   .   .

26. Williams also uses the myth of St. Francis in the magnificent poem *The Mental Hospital Garden* (PB 97–100).

This description is not wholly affirmative. The old man, jumping wildly up and down, calling only to the birds and the trees, is in fact rather ridiculous. Yet his sincerity, warm spontaneity, and ecstatic excitement ring true, and if in Williams' attitude toward him there is a gentle irony, there is also an urgent sympathy. Particularly important in this passage is the association which the poet makes between the Evangelist and illumination. His skull, for example, is described as "glabrous," a word more suggestive than "bald," for it derives from a root meaning "to gleam" or even "to glow." In regard to the theme of the breakdown of language which runs throughout the poem, it is also significant that the Evangelist is described as "beginning to speak."

After another brief fragment from one of the poetess' letters, the Evangelist is described further:

>   —calling with his back
> to the paltry congregation, calling the winds;
> a voice calling, calling . . .
>
>   But as he rests, they sing—when
> prodded—as he wipes his prismed brow.
>   The light
> fondles it as if inclined to form a halo—
> Then he laughs.

As I suggested before, the Evangelist's voice is identified with the Falls of the Passaic. The repeated word "calling" is important in this regard, mainly because it is associated with the Falls' "beckoning."[27] Then, too, both the Evangelist's voice and the Falls are "unheard." The identification between the two "voices" is even more evident in the reference to "his prismed brow." It is, we recall, "late spring" (57:14), or perhaps even "early summer" (see 10:1), and the old man is bareheaded in the sun (83:12–13). As he preaches, beads of

27. Cf. 71:18–25 and 131:8–17.

82

perspiration fall from his brow, reflecting and refracting the light like tiny prisms, imitating the sparkling water as it rushes over the Falls. Later, of course, the identification between the Evangelist's voice and the Falls is made explicit:

—with monotonous insistence
the falls of his harangue hung featureless
upon the ear, yet with a certain strangeness
as if arrested in space.

As I have already mentioned, the curious kind of suspended motion or static process involved here, allied to the timelessness in time of the artistic moment, is the effect one gets when looking at any water- fall. The Evangelist's "prismed brow" is no doubt also meant to emphasize the personal "cost" of his preaching,[28] and this, together with the image of the "halo," seem to associate him with Christ.

If, however, the Evangelist is to some extent a new manifestation of Christ, no clear sign of such significance is apparent: "No figure/ from the clouds seems brought hovering near." His unconvention- ality, in fact, rather humorously frightens off the poor Polock who happens to wander by:

. . . Few listen.
Or, in fact, pay the the least
attention, walking about, unless some Polock
with his mouth open tries to make it out,
as if it were some Devil (looks into the faces
of a young couple passing, laughing
together, for some hint) What kind of priest
is this? Alarmed, goes off scowling, looking
back.

The Polock is clearly aware of the Evangelist's energy (he stares in open-mouthed "wonder" and even tries "to make it out"). But in his conventionality he too quickly assumes that this energy is

28. Cf. 17:1–18.

demonic. The Falls, too, we may recall, involves an energy which is terrifying as well as beautiful, and as we shall see, a primary theme of Book III is that the two qualities are inextricably linked.

The answer to the Polock's question, "What kind of priest/ is this?" is given by the poet almost at once:

> This is a Protestant! protesting—as
> though the world were his own.

These two lines are very rich. On the one hand, the Evangelist is a "Protestant" in the sense that he exists within the tradition which affirms the validity of the individual's "inner light," the tradition which affirms the possibility of man's coming to terms with his world (including his God) directly and without intermediaries. The Evangelist is protesting "as though the world were his own"—and in the sense that it is the world which he approaches concretely, it indeed *is* his world. All this clearly bears on the position of the poet himself, for it is upon the Evangelist's philosophy that the poet's whole aesthetic is based. The poet, in fact, is another "Protestant," not only approaching his world directly through love, but also inventing it through imagination:

> —another,
> twenty feet off, walks his dog absorbedly
> along the wall top—thoughtful of the dog—
> at the cliff's edge above a fifty foot drop   .

This, I take it, is the "man in tweeds" whom Paterson earlier sees combing out the Collie. The combing out is now complete, experience has been dispersed and transfigured through metamorphosis into the existing or imagined work of art which the artist is here contemplating.[29] This brief scene, as an emblem of what can be

29. One might also argue that these lines refer simply to "another" man strolling indifferently through the Park, as unmindful of the Evangelist's voice as are the rest. The presence of the dog, however, seems to suggest somewhat deeper implications.

accomplished through the loving imagination of the artist, functions
as a minor sermon on behalf of the poet's aesthetic, analogous to
and deriving from the major sermon which makes up the bulk of
the section.[30]

The alternation between the Evangelist's "harangue" and his
assistants' "horn blasts" continues, "But his decoys bring in no
ducks—other than/ the children with their dusty little minds/ and
happiest *non sequiturs.*" At this point, however, the Evangelist is
"entranced" and the poet "records" his words at length:

> This is what the preacher said: Don't think
> about me. Call me a stupid old man, that's
> right. Yes, call me an old bore who talks until
> he is hoarse when nobody wants to listen. That's
> the truth. I'm an old fool and I know it.
>
> BUT   .   !
> You can't ignore the words of Our Lord Jesus
> Christ who died on the Cross for us that we
> may have Eternal Life! Amen.

The first line here seems to echo *The Waste Land,* particularly the
section called "What the Thunder Said," but also that called "The
Fire Sermon." Yet the distance between Eliot and Williams is
enormous. Eliot bases his sermon upon three Sanskrit words—
words which, for him, embody the oldest and most profound knowledge of our race. Ultimately, of course, his concern is with the potential contemporary manifestations of these words, but they are seen
as valid primarily because of their antiquity. Williams' sermon is
based only upon the simple idea of love. This idea, to be sure, is no
less ancient and profound than Eliot's "Give, Sympathize, Control"—
it is, as the Evangelist says, "the riches of all the ages"—but the point
is that Williams seeks proof of its validity only in the present. The

30. Cf. the poet's previous "sermon" at 65:8–28.

Evangelist has "seen" the effect of love upon his own life; that such love was taught by Christ two thousand years before does not essentially concern him. His real gospel, that is to say, is not contained in the pat phrases to which his "disciples" (or "assistants") shout "Amen." Rather, it is to be found in the honesty, love, and charity which pervade his entire being. The word "today" which follows the phrase "riches of all the ages" is therefore enormously significant. Eliot is one of "those who know all the Latin and some of the Sanskrit names" (*Grain* 214), but Williams sees resorting to such names, and to the esoteric formulas they embody, as pointless, leading to needless obscurity without any additional dignity or strength. As the Evangelist puts it at almost the beginning of his sermon, the spirit of the Lord

> . . . gives
> the words of even such a plain, ignorant fellow
> as I a touch of His Own blessed dignity and
> and strength among you   .   .[31]

Such dignity and power come primarily from the honesty and vigor of his style. The sentences are generally short and to the point; the diction is colloquial; the syntax is simple and un-Latinate. In short, his language is not "divorced" from the content of his message;[32] it is as humanly "grounded" as is the prose description of Sam Patch in Book I. By way of contrast we might recall the excessively florid and rhetorical style ("Stale as a whale's breath") used by Book I's "minister," Rev. Cumming. Unlike Mr. Cumming and the writer of his story, the Evangelist seems to know only one rhetorical figure—which no doubt he would call simply "emphasis" ("BUT," "GOOD," "NO")—but his naïveté only makes his sincerity

31. Note that Williams has the Evangelist hesitate between the third and fourth lines here. To some extent, this tends to undercut what the Evangelist is saying, but the major effect is, I think, to emphasize his sincerity and conviction.

32. Cf. 21:8–11.

all the more evident. These conclusions are all supported by the fact that Williams writes everything concerning the Evangelist as poetry rather than as prose.

The Evangelist now begins the story of his conversion and subsequent joy. In light of Williams' constant affirmation of the local, that Klaus Ehrens is not native to Paterson by birth might at first seem rather curious. As we will see in regard to the grotesque "Lambert's Castle" of Book III, however, the foreign-born or -made can be local, just as the local-born or -made can be foreign.[33] Klaus tells us that in the Old Country he had become "successful" and "rich" (the two being synonymous in an appropriative society). He wanted to "enjoy" himself and therefore immigrated to America. But when he got here he soon found out that he was "a pretty small frog in a mighty big pool," a pool Williams describes in *In the American Grain* as "the vilest swillhole in christendom" (195).[34]

The origins of this swillhole are to be found in the pervasive materialism which stands behind schemes such as those described in the prose passages now intermingled with the poetry dealing with the Evangelist. The prose items concern various economic schemes to boost the economy of the new republic after the Revolution— Hamilton's plan for the "assumption by the Federal Government of the national debt, and the granting to the government of powers of taxation without which it could not raise the funds necessary for this purpose," and his plans for establishing a "National Manufactory" at "the site of the Great Falls of the Passaic," "a great manufacturing center, a great Federal City, to supply the needs of the country" as well as to ensure "income for taxation"—and with the later creation of the Federal Reserve System. These attacks on "Puritan" institutions will be taken up again, at length, in *Paterson* IV.[35] Stressing as they do our society's ingrained concern with

33. Cf. 19:17–22, 11:7–12, 48:1–13.
34. Strictly speaking, at this point in *In the American Grain* Williams is describing the Passaic River. But as we have seen, his basic symbolism involves an identification between the river and life in the contemporary world.
35. Cf. 213:1–218:18.

money, usury, production, etc., they support the Evangelist's Poundian denunciation of the monetary motive in life:

> ... So
> I went to work all over again. I suppose
> I was born with a gift for that sort of thing.
> I throve and I gloried in it. And I thought then
> that I was happy. And I was — as happy
> as money could make me.
>
> But did it make me GOOD? ...
>
> NO! he shouted, bending
> at the knees and straightening himself up
> violently with the force of his emphasis—like
> Beethoven getting a crescendo out of an
> orchestra—NO!
>
> It did *not* make me good.

Ultimately more important, however, is the Evangelist's very un-
Poundian "answer," his positive affirmation of outgoing generosity
and charity. Williams more or less accepts Pound's diagnosis of
America's economic ills, but he does not accept his contemporary's
overly simplified social and economic cures.

Williams' remedy, love, is therefore developed in the reminder
of the Evangelist's sermon:

> And so
> one day I heard a voice ... a voice—just
> as I am talking to you here today. ...
>
> our blessed Lord came to me and put His hand
> on my shoulder and said, Klaus, you old fool,
> you've been working too hard. You look
> tired and worried. Let me help you.

I am worried, I replied, but I don't know what to
do about it. I got everything that money can
buy but I'm not happy, that's the truth.

And the Lord said to me, Klaus, get rid of your
money. You'll never be happy until you do that.

Like the voice of the Evangelist himself, the voice Klaus Ehrens
hears is associated with the voice of the Falls and with the voice
of the poet; indeed, all these voices are ultimately the same. It might
also be pointed out that Klaus *hears* the voice which is elsewhere
described as being "unheard," just as he *speaks* when speaking is
elsewhere described as being "impossible." What is especially important in this passage is the fact that Klaus' God is a God close to
man. Indeed, when Klaus tells us that *"one day/* our blessed Lord
came to me and *put His hand/ on my shoulder"* (italics mine), we
are reminded of the Rasles figure in *In the American Grain:* "Rasles
lived thirty-four years, October 13, 1689 to October 12, 1723, with
his beloved savages, drawing their sweet like honey, TOUCHING
them every day" (120). As such a God concretely approaches the
world, so man, if he is to be truly human, must approach it as well.[36]

At this point there occurs the second prose fragment concerning
the economic schemes of Alexander Hamilton. It is, I think, a mis-
take to read this as a tribute to the "good" that Hamilton would
have done for his country. Rather, we should see in his "imaginative"
schemes the appropriative, ultimately destructive desire to put the
freely given power of the natural world to pragmatic "use." As
Williams puts it in *In the American Grain:*

Paterson he wished to make capital of the country because
there was waterpower there which to his time and mind seemed

36. One might note that the Evangelist describes the "blessed truth" (i.e.
joy and grace) which he receives after his conversion as "descending" upon
him from God. Williams' choice of this particular word may support the implication that the "descent" which is man's loving and imaginative approach
to his world is a mimesis of actions that are divine.

colossal. And so he organized a company to hold the land thereabouts, with dams and sluices, the origin today of the vilest swillhole in christendom, the Passaic River; impossible to remove the nuisance so tight had he, Hamilton, sewed up his privileges unto kingdomcome, through his holding company, in the State legislature. *His* company. *His* United States: Hamiltonia—the land of the company. . . . once the Revolution over the New World instead of being freed slipped into a tyranny as bad as or worse than the one it left behind . . . of this tyranny, Hamilton was the agent. [195]

Klaus now brings his sermon to its climax:

> Give up my money! . . .
>
>   That would be a hard thing
> for me to do. What would my rich friends say?
> They'd say, That old fool Klaus Ehrens must
> be getting pretty crazy, getting rid of his
> cash. What! give up the thing I'd struggled all
> my life to pile up—so I could say I was rich?
> No! that I couldn't do. But I was troubled
> in mind. . . .
>
>   I couldn't eat, I couldn't
> sleep for thinking of my trouble so that
> when the Lord came to me the third time I was
> ready and I kneeled down before Him
> and said, Lord, do what you will with me!
>
> Give away your money, He said, and I
> will make you the richest man in the world!
> And I bowed my head and said to Him, Yea, Lord.
> And His blessed truth descended upon me and filled
> me with joy, such joy and such riches as I
> had never in my life known to that day and I said
> to Him, Master!

The pattern here is typical, even archetypal, recalling parallels in the Bible (both Old and New Testaments) as well as in myth in general: he who loses one kind of life finds another. Even more important is the parallel to the life of St. Francis of Assisi (as I noted before, that the Evangelist is "calling to the birds and trees" strongly supports this parallel). The "voice" Klaus Ehrens hears and the vision of the Word which "comes to him," then, may be associated with the words of the Gospel which came as a beckoning call to St. Francis: "Freely ye have received, freely give. Provide neither gold, nor silver, nor brass in your purses; Nor scrip for your journey, neither two coats, neither shoes, nor yet staves: for the workman is worthy of his meat" (Matt. 10:8–10). St. Francis, like the Evangelist, went through an initial period of materialistic pleasure in his town, and was in fact the recognized leader of the young men of the town in their revels. Klaus, as he tells us, was "as happy/ as money could make me." Both men responded to their call by profusely giving alms to the poor, and both received in consequence the "great riches" of the local world.

As the Evangelist now begins to fade out of the poem, the poet universalizes him and places him within the larger context of the poem as a whole:

> Is this the only beauty here?
> And is this beauty—
> torn to shreds by the
> lurking schismatists?
>
> Where is beauty among
> these trees?
> Is it the dogs the owners
> bring here to dry their coats?
>
> These women are not
> beautiful and reflect
> no beauty but gross   .   .
> Unless it is beauty

> to be, anywhere,
> so flagrant in desire   .
> The beauty of holiness,
> if this it be,
>
> is the only beauty
> visible in this place
> other than the view
> and a fresh budding tree.

In this lyric three of the major symbols of Book II are gathered together—the new-washed, combed-out Collie; the vulgar but vital women; and most important, the Evangelist himself. What is important is the fact that the Evangelist's "beauty of holiness"—or whatever we are to call it, the poet is not quite sure—incorporates both the beauty associated with the vitality of these women and the beauty associated with the "combing/caressing" performed by the man in tweeds, the Falls, and the poet. The last six lines are a little ambiguous, but basically they seem to mean that such "beauty of holiness," in assimilating the other kinds of "beauty" in the Park, is also at one with the spontaneous beauty and vitality of the natural landscape. The answer to the first stanza's first question—"Is this the only beauty here?"—is therefore yes, but in a sense which paradoxically does not exclude "other" modes of beauty. The answer to the second question—"And *is* this beauty," even in its being "torn to shreds by the/ lurking schismatists?"—like the answers to the remaining rhetorical questions in the lyric, is clearly yes as well.

As Paterson leans on the parapet, "thinking," the poem becomes more and more the record of his stream of consciousness.[37] The Evangelist is still preaching, but his words now join the flow of thoughts in Paterson's mind:

37. The events of the poem are themselves, of course, the stream of consciousness of the sleeping Giant. One may recall the events concerning H. J. Earwicker, and the relationship between Williams and Joyce is in fact pronounced. Of this relationship Parker Tyler writes as follows: "Dr. Williams'

So I started to get rid of my money. It didn't take
me long I can tell you! I threw it away with both
hands. And I began to feel better.

Paterson remembers the hanging of a "cold blooded/ murderer," a
man who, in striking contrast to the Evangelist, had presumably
killed for money. "Groups at various/ vantages along the cliff" had
"gathered since before daybreak" to witness his hanging, and as the
poet observes "the preacher, outnumbered," addressing only "the
leaves in the patient trees," he meditates on the neglect of his
"Master": "The gentle Christ . . . Split between/ Athens and/ the
amphyoxus . . . Weeps and is/ remembered as of/ the open tomb."
   The sequence of alternating poetry and prose that follows grows
out of the image of God's "boundless resources," which the Evangelist uses at the close of his sermon:

           . . . the riches that had been given me are
           beyond all counting. You can throw them
           carelessly about you on all sides—and still
           you will have more.

As I suggested above, the riches Klaus Ehrens receives are the freely
given riches of the world he approaches. Such riches are "beyond all
counting," like the ways in which the protagonist loves the poetess,
both because they are infinite and because they are beyond pragmatic
use. The joy which derives from such riches increases as these riches
are given away, for as love is given to more and more of the world,
those things which are loved become themselves sources of joy.
   Juxtaposed to this passage are prose items dealing with the Federal

---

situation is Finnegans' situation. It is that of the epic, or myth, hero who
dreams his action to the extent that it ceases to be individually his and becomes also that of others" ("The Poet of *Paterson, Book One,*" *Briarcliff
Quarterly,* 3 [1946], 171). In *Paterson* one aspect of the epic/mythic hero
dreams the actions of another aspect of himself.

Reserve System and with the schemes of Alexander Hamilton. The "power" of the Federal Reserve System, as Williams sees it, is a power very different from the power of "God Almighty," but ironically, the sources of the two kinds of power do have some things in common. For example, they both "create" riches out of "nothing" —out of green paper or out of the common things of the world, things which have in themselves no intrinsic value—and they both operate on a system by which the value of what is given increases rather than decreases ("the interest is always greater than the principle"—92:1–2). Since, however, the Federal Reserve System is based on the principles of possession and appropriative exploitation, it is overwhelmingly "Puritan." I have already mentioned how Williams views Hamilton's ideas in general, not as plans for bettering the lot of mankind, but as schemes for selfishly exploiting nature. This conclusion is supported by the clearly deliberate contrasts between the "uselessness" of the Evangelist's doctrine and the "usefulness" of "The Society for Useful Manufactures" which Hamilton would establish, and between the uncountable riches available to the loving Evangelist and the finite and precisely reckoned riches available to "SUM."

In a difficult but powerful lyric at almost the end of Section II, the stream of Paterson's thoughts reaches a climax. Broadly speaking, the passage is both a prayer and a meditation:

> If there is subtlety,
> you are subtle. I beg your indulgence:
> no prayer should cause you anything
> but tears. I had a friend   .   .   .
> let it pass. I remember when as a child
> I stopped praying and shook with fear
> until sleep—your sleep calmed me —

Sister Bernetta has written that it is God "Who is the addressee [here], according to the title given this section in a microfilmed version of the Williams manuscript at the Lockwood Memorial

Library of the University of Buffalo."[38] To some degree, of course, Sister Bernetta's conclusion is undoubtedly correct. It is equally relevant, however, that in all published versions of the passage Williams omitted any explicit identification of the addressee, and one may therefore assume that he did not wish to have the passage limited only to the connotations such an identification would imply. Allied to Sister Bernetta's view, then, yet distinct from it and perhaps more accurate, is the view based on reading the "you" here, not simply as "God," but rather as a broader, more inclusive "principle." Such a principle might also encompass the Evangelist and his message, the Falls and the "myth" behind it, the world of the local and the mythical "genius of the place," the "radiant gist,"[39] and most importantly, what might be called a principle of universal truth and beauty.[40]

In any case, Paterson/Williams here invokes a principle which is merciful ("no prayer should cause you anything but tears") and peace-giving ("your sleep calmed me"). As regards the latter quality, it is significant that Williams carefully distinguishes "your sleep," which is associated with the security of love and with the "creative repose" of art,[41] from "the sleep/ piecemeal," which is associated with "Puritanism." The first sentence of the lyric, at least when taken with the remainder of the poem, may well be another covert reply to Eliot, particularly to the well-known beginning of his "Notes on The Waste Land," where he pompously suggests the erudition requisite to "understanding" his poem. If there is "subtlety" associated with ultimate truth and beauty, Williams replies, such subtlety as Eliot suggests not only in his Notes but also in his general technique, then the addressee of this lyric is also subtle. But as Williams emphasizes again and again, this principle is not so difficult to understand as Eliot supposes, and it can be approached directly, without intermediate aids. So the tone here is almost humorous, a tone sup-

38. Quinn, *Metamorphic Tradition,* p. 109.
39. See Books III and IV.
40. Cf. the "Beautiful thing" of Book III.
41. See my discussion of *Paterson* III, below.

ported by the phrase, "I beg your indulgence," which immediately follows.

In the second stanza the contrast between Williams and Eliot is developed even more explicitly. Almost certainly, its opening sentence is an answer to the passage from Eliot to which I have referred:

> You also, I am sure, have read
> Frazer's Golden Bough. It does you
> justice—a prayer such as might be made
> by a lover who
> appraises every feature of his bride's
> comeliness, and terror—
> terror to him such as one, a man
> married, feels toward his bride—

Eliot's poem, being deliberately remote and obscure, does not, as Williams sees it, do justice to the "you" addressed here. *The Golden Bough,* however, does it justice in at least three ways. In the first place, Frazer's work shows the complexity (one kind of "subtlety") of Williams' "you" by elaborating the myriad of related forms in which it is embodied. In both *The Golden Bough* and Williams' prayer, however, the various aspects of the divine *tend* toward identity. Frazer's work, then, also does justice to the principle addressed in the lyric by suggesting that the principle's complexity may ultimately be a unity. The final way in which *The Golden Bough* does justice to Williams' "you" is by suggesting the impermanence of its natural manifestations. A basic theme of Frazer's study is what he calls the theme of "Dying and Reviving Gods," a cycle applying not only to the individual gods themselves (e.g. Adonis, Dionysus, Christ) but also to the historical sequence of these gods. This aspect of Williams' "god" emerges as most important at the end of the lyric, and to introduce it here is the major function of the stanza's last six lines. "Comeliness/terror" may be linked with "blossoming/ withering," with "composition/decomposition," and with "creation/

destruction." As we have seen in regard to the Falls, and as we will see in regard to the "Beautiful thing" in *Paterson* III, the two sets of qualities are inseparable.

The references to "lover," "bride," and "marriage" in the second stanza clearly involve Williams' basic symbolism. Only the man of love and imagination (the "lover"), that is, can come to terms with ("approach" or "marry") the seemingly disparate aspects of the "you" (the "bride"). The nature of this "you" is further developed in stanza three:

> You are the eternal bride and
> father—quid pro quo,
> a simple miracle that knows
> the branching sea, to which the oak
> is coral, the coral oak.
> The Himalayas and prairies
> of your features amaze and delight—

As we have seen, much the same statement is made at the close of *Paterson* I, where the earth, previously described as a female (presumably both bride and mother), becomes a male as well, the "father of all/ speech." At first glance, this appears curious indeed, but Williams' point is simply that the principle he addresses is not only the object of his quest (the beauty or myth he approaches) but also its source. As usual, the word "eternal" here does not mean "lasting forever," but rather eternal as the "eternal moment" is eternal or as the stones of the grasshopper lyric are eternal ("so long as stone shall last"). In another sense, of course, it also means "recurrent."

The last two lines of this stanza provide the basis for the first part of the next. "The Himalayas and prairies" to which Williams refers are clearly being affirmed as sources of imaginative wonder; all the features of the approached world, of the world which is man's bride and which embodies the source of his being, "amaze and delight" as, traditionally, the features of one's beloved amaze and delight. If the world is full of beauty, however, such beauty is available only to the man of love and imagination. In "reality," the "you" of this lyric has been overthrown, and it will be recovered not in its "real" debacle but only in the individual mind:

> Why should I move from this place
> where I was born? knowing
> how futile would be the search
> for you in the multiplicity
> of your debacle.

Unlike Eliot and Pound, who ran "off toward the peripheries . . . for clarity . . . [and] loveliness" (48:1–9), Williams would "invent" these things in the world of which he is the center.

Deriving from the reference to "comeliness and terror" in stanza two, and the reference to "the multiplicity of your debacle" in stanza four, the remainder of the lyric develops the theme of permanence and impermanence:

> . . . The world spreads
> for me like a flower opening—and
> will close for me as might a rose—
>
> wither and fall to the ground
> and rot and be drawn up
> into a flower again. But you
> never wither—but blossom
> all about me. In that I forget
> myself perpetually—in your
> composition and decomposition
> I find my   .   .
>   despair!

The basic difficulty here lies in the word "that," and it is important to realize that it refers to "your composition and decomposition," to the cycle described in the first sentence of the lines just quoted. The

protagonist's "despair" is only a despair arising from the knowledge
that in the "real" world the manifestations of the permanent principles of beauty, truth, and power are always impermanent—that the
only "permanence" is the permanence of endless recurrence.[42] The
poet, that is, despairs only that the "you" which "never withers" is
transient in the world of common reality. There is, however, another kind of permanence, the permanence of the eternal moment,
which brings man into contact with the eternity of these principles.
Such an eternity transcends the world of common reality, and in this
eternity the poet can only rejoice. What the poet is saying at the
end of this lyric, then, is that he "despairs" only when he "forgets
himself," when he ceases to have faith in the salvation of love and
imagination. When this faith is maintained, he finds "a reversal of
despair."

The section concludes with yet another excerpt from the poetess'
letters. Placed appropriately after the word "despair," it contains
passages such as the following:

I have been feeling (with that feeling increasingly stronger)
that I shall never again be able to recapture any sense of my
own personal identity (without which I cannot write, of course
—but in itself far more important than the writing) until I
can recapture some faith in the reality of my own thoughts and
ideas and problems which were turned into dry sand by your
attitude toward those letters and by that note of yours later.

There is, to be sure, great urgency here. The poetess seems on the
verge of a fate similar to that of a suicide described somewhat
earlier: "The detectives found a note on the kitchen table addressed
to a soldier from Fort Bragg, N. C. The contents of the letter showed
that she was in love with the soldier, the detective said" (82:16–18).
Yet the pathos of her situation does not alter the fact that, to a large
extent, she has precipitated it herself.

42. See 22:19–23:19.

THE DESCENT BECKONS

The third section of *Paterson* II begins with a terse, almost epigrammatic lyric on the negative principle which is the contrary to all that the poet has previously affirmed. Placed as it is, directly after the excerpt from the poetess' letters at the end of the second section, this passage functions as a kind of judgment on the letters, its relatively cold precision offsetting the pity which the letters are beginning more and more to arouse. Like the opening lines of Section II, then, this lyric operates to establish what the section will react *against;* it does not function as a statement of the section's theme.

The passage itself is rather obscure:

> Look for the nul
> defeats it all
>
> The N of all
> equations   .
>
> that rock, the blank
> that holds them up
>
> which pulled away—
> the rock's
>
> their fall. Look
> for that nul
>
> that's past all
> seeing
>
> the death of all
> that's past
>
> all being   .

The first "Look" here seems primarily to mean "Watch out!" or "Keep your eyes open!," the preposition "for" which follows it seeming to mean "because." In another possible reading, "Look" would mean "Search," "nul" would be the object of "for," and the entire first line would be the subject of "defeats." The "nul" is clearly that principle which negates everything positive, which defeats or holds to no account every aspect of the "you" that the poet celebrates just before. It is also "Abstraction," upon which men, denying the value of individual "things" or of that which cannot be "formulated," construct their pragmatic, use-oriented equations.

At the end of *Paterson* I we read of "the myth/ that holds up the rock." Here in *Paterson* II we read of a very different kind of support—"that rock" which is simply the massive body of "Puritan" forms and conventions, a rock that is paradoxically a "blank." This negative mass supports not the positive matter symbolically dispersed by the Falls, but only the undifferentiated "they"[43] which Williams would call the "great beast." The men making up this amorphous mass are fragmented ("piecemeal"), not unlike the shored up ruins of the protagonist at the end of *The Waste Land,* and if the negation holding them up should be "pulled away," they would simply fall apart. The phrase "holds them up," however, has other meanings as well. Quite literally, in terms of Williams' symbolism, the principle of negation prevents men from "falling," in the "descent" which is paradoxically their salvation, holding them up when they should "drown" or "sink." "That rock" thus robs (yet another meaning of "holds up") men of their true redemption, and it is their "fall" in the sense that it separates them from the "Falls." It should be evident, then, that "the nul" is not, as Sister Bernetta seems to think, the woman or rock of imagination and love.[44] It is, on the contrary, the very negation of these, and if it is to be associated with woman at all, it would have to be women like the poetess, like the "She" who appears at this section's end, or like the "legalists" of

43. "They" also refers to "equations."
44. Quinn, pp. 110 ff.

Book III.[45] The nul is "past all/ seeing" both because it is not a concrete thing and because it is totally divorced from even the simplest mode of artistic contemplation. Approach leads to a being which is "past all being," but of such being the nul is only "the death."[46]

In spite of negation, however, the positive will still survive:

> But Spring shall come and flowers will bloom
> and man must chatter of his doom   .   .

On first reading this couplet, the last line seems to conflict with the first. But if Spring comes and flowers blossom, both will eventually pass away, and similarly, if man must chatter in fear of death, he may also sing in celebration of life. In the lyric at the end of the previous section, it is of course this cycle in which the protagonist finds his "despair." Here, however, his feeling is considerably less ambivalent: not only does he begin the thought with the word "But"; he also refuses to acknowledge its graver undertones by merely passing it off in a couplet, the insignificance of which is suggested by its glibness even as its inevitability is suggested by its rhyme. In any case, the "eternity" with which the poet is ultimately concerned is a different order of eternity altogether, a blossoming which is eternal because it is in the imagination.

The passage which now occurs Williams reprinted in 1954 (with only a few minor changes in punctuation) as *The Descent,* the first poem of *The Desert Music and Other Poems.*[47] For the most part, of course, this poem is written in the triadic stanza and "measured line" which eventually became the staple of Williams' verse. It was,

---

45. See 169:13–18.

46. The ideas here are very close to the ideas of Wallace Stevens' *Mrs. Alfred Uruguay:* "And for her,/ To be, regardless of velvet, could never be more/ Than to be, she could never differently be,/ Her no and no made yes impossible."

47. See also *PB* 73–74.

indeed, specifically this passage which precipitated Williams' later technical development:

> *Paterson II* is a milestone for me. One of the most successful things in it is a passage in section three of the poem [96:1–97:15 is quoted] which brought about—without realizing it at the time of writing—my final conception of what my own poetry should be; a passage which, sometime later, brought all my thinking about free verse to a head. . . . From the time I hit on this I knew what I was going to have to do.[48]

The content of this poem is as important as its form. It opens with an affirmation of the descent:

> The descent beckons
> > as the ascent beckoned
> > > Memory is a kind
>
> of accomplishment
> > a sort of renewal
> > > even
>
> an initiation, since the spaces it opens are new
> places
> > inhabited by hordes
> > > heretofore unrealized,
>
> of new kinds—
> > since their movements
> > > are towards new objectives
>
> (even though formerly they were abandoned).

It is important to realize that memory here is equivalent to the eternal present, or, perhaps more accurately, involves a bringing over of the past into the imagination's eternal present. In *Asphodel*,

---

48. *I Wanted To Write a Poem,* ed. Edith Heal (Boston, Beacon Press, 1958), pp. 80–82.

That Greeny Flower, addressing his wife, Williams expresses the
same idea as follows:

> We lived long together
> > a life filled,
> > > if you will,
> with flowers. . . .
> > > Today
> I'm filled with the fading memory of those flowers
> > that we both loved . . .
> When I was a boy
> > I kept a book
> > > to which, from time
> to time,
> > > I added pressed flowers
> > > > until, after a time,
> I had a good collection. . . .
> > > I bring you,
> > > > reawakened,
> a memory of those flowers.   [PB 153–55]

The "descent," then, on one level, is a descent into an ever-present
past, into the ever-living life of the imagination.[49] Such a descent
"beckon*s*" (cf. 71:19, etc.) in the present as much as the original
experience (ascent) "beckon*ed*" in the past. For as a revitalization
of experience, memory is itself a variety of that experience. In
bringing the particulars of the past over into the present, moreover,

49. I find myself echoing Blake, and the passage I am thinking of is
worth quoting. Writing to George Cumberland on Apr. 12, 1827, just four
months before his death, Blake says, "I have been very near the gates of
death, and have returned very weak and an old man, feeble and tottering,
but not in spirit and life, not in the real man, the imagination, which liveth
for ever." The passage from *Asphodel, That Greeny Flower* which I have
taken as my first epigraph is remarkably similar to this.

the imagination metamorphoses them into something new, "even though formerly they were abandoned."

                    . . . A

   world lost,
            a world unsuspected
                    beckons to new places
   and no whiteness (lost) is so white as the memory
   of whiteness   .

The spaces in the mind that such a revitalized and transfigured memory opens are peopled by new thoughts—thoughts "heretofore unrealized," not only because a kind of recollection and re-collection in tranquility allows more time for imaginatively grasping more of the memory's particulars, but also because subsequent experience will necessarily modify and supplement the past. I touched on another example of this when discussing the grasshopper lyric in Section I, for when the memory of the "grasshopper of red-basalt" from Chapultepec "tumbles from the core of [Paterson's] mind," it merges with, and is consequently altered by, the various real and imagined grasshoppers churring all about him.

Ultimately more important than the descent into memory, however, is the descent to the concrete particulars of the local. As I have said, the past, when brought over into the present, is a part of this local, but it is only a part. The descent to the local ground beckons to Williams as the ascent to foreign forms and ideas beckoned to Pound and Eliot—indeed, as the ascent beckoned to all the conventionally "poetic" poets of the past. The new vistas it opens to such a man, as suggested by the grasshopper lyric and by the prose account of the lake-draining in Book I (46:28–47:37), are the previously "unrealized" vistas of a newly "invented" world.

In the remainder of this sequence the poet meditates on the fact that the descent is as likely to end in despair and defeat as in triumph and success:

No defeat is made up entirely of defeat—since
the world it opens is always a place
      formerly
           unsuspected....
The descent
      made up of despairs
           and without accomplishment
realizes a new awakening   :
           which is a reversal
of despair.

           For what we cannot accomplish, what
is denied to love,
      what we have lost in the anticipation—
          a descent follows,
endless and indestructible.

The "despair" involved in these lines is complex. Most simply, it is the despair that a pragmatic accomplishment has *not* been made. Ultimately, however, this is unimportant, for it is only to the "Puritan" that the works of love and imagination have no value. To some degree, then, the despair felt by the protagonist is the despair traditionally felt by anyone questing after transcendent goals: one kind of life must be lost in order that another might be attained. On a deeper level the despair here is the despair that, in the "real" world, the works of love and imagination are impermanent, the despair that the cycle of perpetual birth and death must necessarily be cyclic. This kind of despair is overcome by the poet's faith that through the imagination the eternities behind the cycle may be made accessible to man within the "eternal moment." Most important of all, it is the inevitable despair in the knowledge that there is a limit to what the descent will accomplish, at least in the face of what we "anticipate." Love and imagination are human qualities, and, like everything human, the degree to which they lead man toward transcending the human, or as Williams might prefer to put it, in attaining to the truly human, is necessarily limited. Moreover, because even the effort to attain to such a position involves an enormous strain, even what love and imagination *can* accomplish they can accomplish only momentarily. This is a version of the so-called paradox of the Romantic imagination, the paradox which not even the great Romantics, at least the more Promethean ones, could finally sustain. Here, of course, Williams is not a Promethean. Nevertheless, he both accepts the challenge of a difficult quest and affirms at least the possibility that it can be fulfilled.

The idea that the descent "realizes a new awakening" only in a time of apparent despair is carried further in the beautiful lines which occur at about the middle of this lyric:

> With evening, love wakens
>   though its shadows
>   which are alive by reason
> of the sun shining—
>   grow sleepy now and drop away
>   from desire   .
>
> Love without shadows stirs now
>   beginning to waken
>   as night
> advances.

Night is traditionally the time of love, just as it is traditionally the time of imagination. This Romantic usage does not, of course, imply that nighttime love is necessarily furtive or surreptitious, and on the contrary, the "shadows" of ambiguity and restraint are here associated with the day.[50] Tellingly, however, soon no one will be in the park but "guilty lovers and stray dogs," for "At nine o'clock the park closes. You/ must be out of the lake, dressed, in/ your cars and going." Reminding us of the "couriers to the ceremonial of

50. Cf. Shelley's *To Night*.

love" in Section I, "the crickets'/ black wings and hylas wake," but the loveless, unimaginative " 'great beast' [is] all removed/ before the plunging night" which it fears.

Paterson (as Faitoute) now hears the sound of the waterfall ("Listen! —/ the pouring water!"), but the noise of the indifferent crowd, fleeing from the darkness, virtually drowns it out ("A/ departing car scatters gravel as it/ picks up speed!"). "The dogs," at first probably poets,[51] "and trees," symbols of the vitality and beauty of the world, "conspire to invent/ a world" of art, either imagined or actually created. But such a world is "gone!"—"abandoned" by the crowd and hence unavailable to them. They are themselves reduced to "dogs" and "trees," in the sense of "beasts" and "vegetables," as Williams writes some of the most scathing lines in the poem:

> Outworn! *le pauvre petit ministre*
> did his best, they cry,
> but though he sweat for all his worth
> no poet has come   .
>
> Bow, wow! Bow, wow!
>
> Variously the dogs barked, the trees
> stuck their fingers to their noses. No
> poet has come, no poet has come.

The irony, of course, is that a poet *has* come. Like the Evangelist with whom he is so clearly associated, he may sweat for all his worth,[52] but unlike the Evangelist, he is not even recognized as *"le pauvre petit ministre"* trying to do his best. Faitoute "rejects him finally/ and strolls off," but this is not, of course, a rejection of "reconciliation" and "approach."

At this point there occurs a passage describing both what Williams

51. Cf. 11:7–16.
52. Cf. 81:15–17 and 88:1–7.

values and what he despises, not in "poetry" but in "the poem."[53]
The first part of the passage describes what he values:

> That the poem,
> the most perfect rock and temple, the highest
> falls, in clouds of gauzy spray, should be
> so rivaled.

These symbols, except for the "temple," have all occurred before.
The "rock" is the rock which symbolizes love, beauty, and imagination, the rock supporting the Park and the Falls, the "stone endlessly in flight." The "temple" seems to be a kind of shrine for the
Evangelist's love and for the poet's imagination, and it is no doubt
meant to contrast to the "Church" discussed above. The Falls, of
course, is a symbol of the energy of the eternal present, the gauzy
spray symbolizing the particulars of experience which that energy
"disperses" prior to the transfiguring metamorphosis.

The remainder of this passage concerns that which "rivals"
Williams' ideal:

> . . . that the poet,
> in disgrace, should borrow from erudition (to
> unslave the mind): railing at the vocabulary
> (borrowing from those he hates, to his own
> disfranchisement)   .
> —discounting his failures   .
> seeks to induce his bones to rise into a scene,
> his dry bones, above the scene, (they will not)
> illuminating it within itself, out of itself
> to form the colors, in the terms of some
> back street, so that the history may escape
> the panders.

53. In keeping with Williams' insistence on local particulars. "I never if
possible speak of poetry," he writes in a letter to Henry Wells (Apr. 12,
1950, in *Selected Letters*, p. 286).

This is clearly yet another attack on the poetics of an Eliot or a Pound. Although both poets "borrow from erudition," this seems to be primarily an allusion to the poetry of Eliot ("dry bones" are important not only in *The Waste Land* but also in *Ash-Wednesday* and a number of his other poems). "Borrowing from those he hates, to his own/ disfranchisement" seems to be an allusion to the constant "railing" of Pound. Whether his diatribe is directed against "the vocabulary," "Usury," "the ambulating dunghill FDR" (254: 11–12), or "the offering da shittad aaabull instead of history" (255:6), his scurrilous language, Williams suggests, tends only to destroy the effectiveness of his poetry.

As for Paterson himself, he would "accomplish the inevitable" —that is, approach the "poor, the invisible, thrashing, breeding/ .   debased city." Yet this approach is truly difficult, for the city is

> .   reversed in the mirror of its
> own squalor, debased by the divorce from learning,
> its garbage on the curbs, its legislators
> under the garbage, uninstructed, incapable of
> self instruction   .

To be divorced from learning, to Williams, is to be separated from the teachings of love,[54] and as the "great beast" is "uninstructed" in this regard, so is it incapable of the kind of self-instruction which is affirmed at *Paterson* II's beginning (Paterson "instructs his thoughts" upon the "body" of his world.) In this "divorced" and "debased" city, as in the Park in which the "great beast" has been seeking its pleasures, women are "shallow," men "steadfastly refusing—at the best," and "the language" only "words without style." The approach to the world, then, is hardly inviting or comforting— indeed, it may even seem "rather a nail in the skull." But as Paterson stands "beside the water" of the Falls, "Caught (in mind)," looking down and listening to its roar, even though in some sense he "dis-

54. Cf. 28:6–12.

covers, still, no syllable in the confused/ uproar: missing the sense
(though he tries)"—even so,

> Only the thought of the stream comforts him,
> its terrifying plunge, inviting marriage—and
> a wreath of fur   .

There now begins a dialogue between Paterson and a voice
identified only as "She":

> And She   —
>
> > Stones invent nothing, only a man invents.
> > What answer the waterfall? filling
> > the basin by the snag-toothed stones?
>
> And He   —
>
> > Clearly, it is the new, uninterpreted, that
> > remoulds the old, pouring down   .
>
> And She   —
>
> > It has not been enacted in our day!

This "She" seems to be the voice of the world which the poet must
"marry," but it is a sinister voice, the voice of what Robert Graves
has called a "white goddess."[55] As the poet says, the vital "new"
which "remoulds the old" is "uninterpreted." He is referring, of
course, both to *"Le/ pauvre petit ministre,* swinging his arms,
drown[ing]/ under the indifferent fragrance of the bass-wood trees,"
and to himself. When "She" replies categorically, "It has not been
enacted in our day!," her inability or refusal to see that "It" (invention, approach, interpretation, and reinterpretation) has been
enacted by the poet is similar to the poetess' inability or refusal to
acknowledge how many ways she is loved by "Dr. P." Williams does,

55. At least in the more destructive aspects of such a figure. See Northrop
Frye, *Anatomy of Criticism* (Princeton, 1957), p. 323.

in fact, actually seem to associate the two figures, for at just this point he places another excerpt from the poetess' letters.

Paterson's "anger mounts," then, and "He is chilled to the bone," not only because "he sees squirming roots trampled/ under the foliage of his mind by the holiday/ crowds,"[56] and because he sees the departure of "the Evangels," but also because he is plagued by a voice which becomes more and more sinister in its misunderstanding demands. What "She" says is certainly true:

> Poet, poet! sing your song, quickly! or
> not insects but pulpy weeds will blot out
> your kind. . . .
>
> Marry us! Marry us!
>   Or! be dragged down, dragged
> under and lost . . .
>
> Be reconciled, poet, with your world, it is
> the only truth!

—but the over-insistence with which she says such things throws her motives into question ("at the magic sound of the stream/ she threw herself upon the bed—/ a pitiful gesture!"). "She," like the poetess, wants more than the poet can give without losing his identity. In his extremity he recalls Mrs. Cumming's probable suicide in Book I:

> and leaped (or fell) without a
> language, tongue-tied
>   the language worn out   .

56. "The foliage of his mind" is a phrase which is richly suggestive. Wallace Stevens, in *Credences of Summer,* speaks of "an eternal foliage" which is to be filled "with arrested peace." Keats, in the *Ode to Psyche,* creates a bower "In some untrodden region of my mind,/ Where branched thoughts, now grown with pleasant pain,/ Instead of pines shall murmur in the wind." Keats was, of course, the first important influence on Williams.

—a passage similar to this passage, which occurs just before:

> She was married with empty words:
>> better to
>> stumble at
>> the edge
>> to fall
>> fall
>> and be
>
>> —divorced

The sentence (note typography) cannot be finished; the complete surrender of one's being, "over-marriage" as it were, is only a mode of death-in-life; indeed, it is the ultimate mode of "divorce":[57]

>> —divorced
>
> from the insistence of place—
>> from knowledge,
> from learning—the terms
> foreign, conveying no immediacy, pouring down.
>
>> —divorced
> from time (no invention more), bald as an
> egg   .

To the horror of such a destiny Paterson almost succumbs: "From his eyes sparrows start and/ sing. His ears are toadstools, his fingers have/ begun to sprout leaves (his voice is drowned/ under the falls) . . . He all but falls." But though the "She" continues to challenge him—"Go home. Write. Compose. . . . You have abandoned me!"—Paterson at last escapes from the death-in-life she knowingly

57. Cf. 129:20–130:5.

or unknowingly offers: "He fled pursued by the roar." Discussing this sequence, Sister Bernetta suggests that the poet "flees from the demands for marriage made by the imagination (feminine principle of the universe), answering her call with anger rather than love: 'Faitoute ground his heel/ hard upon the stone.' "[58] It seems to me, however, that neither Paterson nor the female voice can be dismissed quite so easily. The lines:

> Invent (if you can) discover or
> nothing is clear—will surmount
> the drumming in your head. There will be
> nothing clear, nothing clear   .

may well apply to the poet, but they must also apply to the "She" which is a symbol of most of the modern world.

But *Paterson* II is not meant to end pessimistically, as Williams wittily indicates by inserting an optimistic weather report: "Sunny today, with the highest temperature near 80 degrees; moderate southerly winds. Party cloudy and continued warm tomorrow, with moderate southerly winds." There now occur a few fragmentary lines affirming once again the ultimate power of love:

> Her belly   .   her belly is like
> a cloud   .   a cloud
>   at evening   .

> His mind would reawaken:

He   Me with my pants, coat and vest still on!

She   And me still in my galoshes!

The subjunctive mood of the fourth line here suggests that the affirmation is somewhat tentative, but as the opening lines of the

58. Quinn, *Metamorphic Tradition*, p. 111.

section make clear, "the descent follows the ascent—to wisdom/ *as to despair*" (italics mine). The "He" and "She" are presumably the same voices we have been dealing with all along, but now they appear to have attained to a certain degree of harmony. In particular, the feminine principle seems to have lost her appropriativeness. Since approaching her is no longer an entrapment, the descent may again be affirmed:[59]

> to the bases; base! to the screaming dregs,
> to have known the clean air .
> From that base, unabashed, to regain
> the sun kissed summits of love!

The poetry of *Paterson* II may therefore conclude with a beautiful lyric celebrating love. According to the lines that introduce it, it is "a song written/ previously," which the poet is "saying over to himself" after composition. It is important to note, however, that this is another example of the past being brought over into the present. Tellingly, the form of this "song" suggests that of the sonnet, a traditional mode for the poetry of love:

> On this most voluptuous night of the year
> the term of the moon is yellow with no light
> the air's soft, the night bird has
> only one note, the cherry tree in bloom

59. Regarding these last dozen or so lines, one could also argue that Paterson comes to accept the "descent" *in spite of* his knowledge that approaching this principle will involve entrapment and the loss of personal identity. Vivienne Koch seems to have this in mind when she writes that the "poet resolves to 'regain/ the sun kissed summits of love!' *even though* the means involve a descent 'to the screaming dregs' " (*Williams*, p. 142; italics mine). As the text stands, however, it seems to me that the "She" here does change and that although Paterson gives himself to the less appropriative version of this principle, he does not give himself to the more appropriative version. This interpretation seems to be reinforced by the parallel which exists between the earlier "She" and the poetess. Miss Koch's argument makes no mention of this parallel.

makes a blur on the woods, its perfume
no more than half guessed moves in the mind.
No insect is yet awake, leaves are few.
In the arching trees there is no sleep.

The blood is still and indifferent, the face
does not ache nor sweat soil nor the
mouth thirst. Now love might enjoy its play
and nothing disturb the full octave of its run.

Her belly   .   her belly is like a white cloud   .   a
white cloud at evening   .   before the shuddering night!

The events of Book II take place in "late spring," and it would appear that Paterson's "sonnet" was written just before. The natural world is reviving after the winter's "piecemeal" sleep, yet it is before the stifling summer heat which will pervade *Paterson* III. That it is night also suggests an awakening of natural vitality, for as we read toward the beginning of the section, love begins "to waken/ as night/ advances" (97:1–4). Now love might enjoy its recreative and re-creative play, with nothing obstructing the full range ("run") of its freedom and exuberance.

The time, then, is ripe for love, but the consummation of "the shuddering night" does not come to pass. As we have seen, the crowd itself is already "all removed/ before the plunging night," and even of his protagonist the most Williams is willing to say is that a consummation *might* now take place ("His mind *would* reawaken"). If fulfillment is deliberately suspended, however, the celebration of love is not itself undercut, and one may still leave *Paterson* II with a feeling that fulfillment is not only possible but imminent. I say "leave" advisedly. This "sonnet" is not, of course, the real conclusion of the book, for there follows a kind of extended postscript in the form of yet another letter from "C.," this time some eight pages in length. These letters, however, only elaborate, in great detail, the various aspects I have already discussed: the pathos of the poetess' situation and her real physical and spiritual poverty, the degree to which Dr. P.'s failure to respond to her is a failure of love, a separation of "literature" from "life," and the poetess' false posturing and her identity-destroying appropriativeness. To suggest this threat of sapping her correspondent's energy is of course one reason why Williams has made this sequence of letters so long. By forcing such a tedious sequence upon the reader, at the very end of more than a hundred pages of difficult material, Williams creates an impatience with the poetess which becomes ever more stifling the more her letters are read. Very soon, in fact, one tends to skip these letters, particularly the last, altogether—especially if one is reading from the edition of *Paterson* II published in 1948, for there these letters are not even connected to the remainder of the poem. This effect, which the poet seems to create deliberately, tends to make the sonnet, not the string of letters, *Paterson* II's functional conclusion.

3.

The Library:

PATERSON, BOOK THREE

A SONG TO MAKE DEATH TOLERABLE

Paterson III begins with a brief meditative lyric introducing the "cost" motif, particularly as it is related to Williams' ideal of aesthetic apprehension. Two voices seem to be involved here, one the voice of the epic protagonist and the other the voice of all that would restrain or vulgarize his quest. Shelley, in *A Defense of Poetry*, writes that "Poetry, and the principle of Self, of which money is the visible incarnation, are the God and Mammon of the world." In modern times, with a tone remarkably akin to that of Shelley or Blake at their most prophetic, Ezra Pound cries out that "With Usura . . . no picture is made to endure nor to live with/ but it is made to sell and sell quickly," and that Usura, further, "lyeth/ between the young bride and her bridegroom/ CONTRA NATU-RAM" *(Canto XLV)*.[1] Shelley's "principle of Self," Pound's "Usura," and the pragmatically objecting voice in Williams' opening lyric

1. Cf. Williams' parody in *Paterson* IV, 213:1–218:18, as well as the passage at 65:8–28, which I have already discussed.

are all related to what I have already described as the "appropriative" view of life. In each case there is an underlying assumption that the pursuit of what is not immediately and pragmatically useful is necessarily contemptible and vain. Paterson, in the midst of his quest for truth and beauty, makes the statement:

> I love the locust tree
> the sweet white locust.

The voice of pragmatic objection asks only "How much?" Paterson seems somewhat surprised that such a question could even enter his mind, and would probably interpret its ambiguous wording to mean simply, "How much do you love the locust tree?" But the question cannot be evaded, and it is mockingly and explicitly re-stated:

> How much does it cost
> to love the locust tree
> in bloom?

The implication is that the cost of love ("relationship") is too high. Nonetheless, the returns are evident to those who wish to see them ("The poem moves them or/ it does not move them"—122:26–27). The writing of poetry is itself a mode of love, and the beautiful lines

> the shelving green
> locust
> whose bright small leaves
> in June
> lean among flowers
> sweet and white

are consequently Williams' imaginative answer to the questioner's objections.

The important section that occurs after this introductory lyric
brings us to the themes centered upon libraries and books:

> A cool of books
> will sometimes lead the mind to libraries
> of a hot afternoon, if books can be found
> cool to the sense to lead the mind away.

The cool of the library offers relief from the heat of the afternoon,
yet as we shall see somewhat later, heat is an agent of positive good
in the poem, being associated with the creative/destructive fire
which sweeps over Paterson in Section II. Further, although the
library is sought as an escape from the stifling oppression of the heat,
the oppresison found within is ultimately worse. On one level the
library is a symbol of memory, a repository of past thoughts; on
another level it is associated with past actions, with past modes of
living and writing. But Williams affirms neither Wordsworthian
consolation through memory nor Poundian/Eliotic faith in traditional cultural and literary forms. Both are deceptive, and both "lead
the mind away" from the roaring and burning present affirmed at the
conclusion of the book.

That the "cool" of the library is deceptive is suggested especially
by the lines,

> For there is a wind or ghost of a wind
> in all books echoing the life
> there, a high wind that fills the tubes
> of the ear until we think we hear a wind,
> actual   .
>
> > to lead the mind away.

The remoteness to modern man of the "life" books ostensibly record
is enormous. What is actually to be found there is only a wind, or
even a ghost of a wind, merely *"echoing* the life/ *there"* (italics
mine), a life in itself to be differentiated from the life which is
ultimately "real." As Williams puts it toward the end of Section II:

> We read: not the flames
> but the ruin left
> by the conflagration
>
> Not the enormous burning
> but the dead (the books
> remaining).[2]

"Drawn from the streets" of the city, which is "a part of nature" as well as "a second body for the human mind" (116), we break off the "seclusion" the mind enjoys when directly contemplating the objects of such a "nature," and "are taken up by/ the books' winds," innumerable intermediaries between the mind and the thing itself. Williams' wording here is important. The mind is most "secluded" when it is amid the streets of the present (being at one with its locale), most oppressed when it is surrounded by the ghosts of the past.

Still, the deceptiveness of the library is not easily to be avoided. We are forever

> . . . seeking, seeking
> down the wind
> until we are unaware which is the wind and
> which the wind's power over us   .
>   to lead the mind away
>
> and there grows in the mind
> a scent, it may be, of locust blossoms
> whose perfume is itself a wind moving
>   to lead the mind away.

2. This is somewhat different from Shelley's famous statement in *A Defence of Poetry*, that "when composition begins, inspiration is already on the decline, and the most glorious poetry that has ever been communicated to the world is probably a feeble shadow of the original conceptions of the

Beauty under such circumstances must clearly be as illusory as truth: the (mere) scent of locust blossoms which grows in the mind is only a wind.

At this point a recollection of the Falls brings Paterson "back to his own/ mind"—that is, back to the living present. The "present pouring down: the roar,/ the roar of the present" is "of necessity" his "sole concern" (172:13), for only in the present is it possible to unravel and comb into straight lines the continuous flow of experience in order to isolate its components and apprehend their beauty. Indeed, it is only in the present that even the simple apprehension/ creation of the opening lyric can exist.

The reminder that beauty is to be found only in the present is followed by the first of many apostrophes to a "Beautiful thing":

> Beautiful thing,
> my dove, unable and all who are windblown,
> touched by the fire
> and unable,
> a roar that (soundless) drowns the sense
> with its reiteration
> unwilling to lie in its bed
> and sleep and sleep, sleep
> in its dark bed.

"Beauty" is inseparable from "things," and the dove, fire, and Falls are all, of course, examples of *beautiful* things. It is the metaphoric implications of these things, however, that are most important, for through the image of the dove, the "Beautiful thing" is associated with peace and love, while through the images of fire and Falls, it is associated with creative/destructive vital energy.

The identification of the "Beautiful thing" with falling water and fire can leave no doubt as to the point of the lines which follow:

---

poet." Williams is thinking, I believe, more in terms of repressive modes of writing, dead language, stale forms, and unimaginative readers.

> Books will give rest sometimes against
> the uproar of water falling
> and righting itself to refall filling
> the mind with its reverberation
> > shaking stone.

The "rest" provided by books immediately recalls the thrice-repeated "sleep" a few lines before. The image of falling and refalling water (also occurring just before) introduces an identity Williams establishes between water and fire. In Section II we read:

> the waterfall of the
> flames, a cataract reversed, shooting
> upward (what difference does it make?).

This identity is a means by which the poet can enrich the suggestiveness of both fire and falls, and it is in itself a symbol of a cycle of perpetual present (cf. the serpent with its tail in its mouth in Book V).

The logical end of the process I have been describing is to be found in the prophetic call for a creative/destructive apocalypse:

> Blow! So be it. Bring down! So be it. Consume
> and submerge! So be it. Cyclone, fire
> and flood. So be it. Hell, New Jersey, it said
> on the letter. Delivered without comment.
> So be it!

The repeated "So be it!" operates as do similar refrains in a biblical prophet like Amos. The library may be a sanctuary to our fears, a place of a repose that is ever the same, but the perverseness of such a sanctuary has been amply indicated. It may "shield us from loneliness," but what Williams affirms is the "solitude" that paradoxically involves communion with the world.

Inside the library, passively "eased" instead of actively "breathless," Paterson turns to an impossible "task": "finding" and "seeking" the "Beautiful thing" in "old newspaper files" and other documents of the past. The words "finding" and "seeking" are weighted, how-ever, for as examples throughout the poem illustrate, vital beauty can be "found" only as it is "created" through an act of aesthetic ap-prehension. At any rate, as Paterson reads of "a child burned in a field," of a pair of lovers "Drowned," "clasped in each others' arms/ (clasped also by the water)," he seems only partially aware that his disposing in the poem, even of material he regards as "wordless," paradoxically endows it, or re-endows it, with a kind of life. "Life," that is, may be absent from the newspaper accounts themselves, but the use of such accounts in a "poem" may "Bring the mind back (attendant upon/ the page) to the day's heat" (152:3–4). Such a process, of course, is ultimately a means of bringing over the past into the present.

The episode which follows is one of Williams' most explicit statements that appropriative, use-oriented materialism is diametri-cally opposed to both poetry and love:

> The "Castle" too to be razed. So be it. For no
> reason other than that it is *there,* in-
> comprehensible; of no USE!

The "too" here may link the episode to the other "murders" of the section (the killing of "the last wolf," the slaughter of the "savages" accused of killing the pigs, the killing of the "little dog" who "never hurt anybody")—all episodes involving destruction of the local. That the Castle *is* a part of the local scene, bizarre as it may appear, Williams stresses first by giving us a brief history of its builder— "Lambert, the poor English boy,/ the immigrant who . . . was the first/ to oppose the unions," and whose head was "full of castles"— and then by describing specific structural details of the building it-self, built

> . . . on the alluvial silt, the rock-fall skirt-
> ing the volcanic upthrust of the "Mountain"

                    —some of the windows
of the main house illuminated by translucent
laminae of planed pebbles (his first wife
admired them) by far the most authentic detail
of the place; at least the best
to be had there and the best artifact   .

The Castle is another example of a "Beautiful thing"—especially
since its obviously eccentric architecture reflects the individualism
of its builder. Both in itself and as a symbol of the human, it embodies the kind of native vigor and energy that Williams sees in the
wolf and in the Indians. Considering Williams' work in general,
of course, the beauty of the local need not always be the beauty of
the exuberant; indeed, the beauty of the *Locust Tree in Flower*
(*CEP* 93) or of *The Red Wheelbarrow* (*CEP* 277) is the beauty of
a vital quietness. But in *Paterson* at least, if exuberance is beauty, the
reverse is usually true as well.

The beauty of exuberance, however, in which the creative borders
dangerously on the destructive, is the beauty most feared by unimaginative man. Thus, in the sequence which follows, the "Beautiful thing" is repeatedly opposed to the tyranny of the "wadded
library":

                . . . Faitoute, his ears
ringing   .   no sound   .   no great city,
as he seems to read—

                    a roar of books
from the wadded library oppresses him
                                        until
his mind begins to drift   .

            Beautiful thing:

                —a dark flame,
a wind, a flood—counter to all staleness.

As in the previous passage about the "Beautiful thing," the symbol is defined through its associations with the book's three catastrophes, all of which are manifestations of an energy which contrasts with the library's repressiveness. Dead men's dreams, the undying spirits of men's minds, although confined by the "walls" of the books and the library, seek an escape through Faitoute. They languish in their tomblike prisons, however, "not from lack of innate ability,"

> but from that which immures them pressed here
> together with their fellows, for respite   .

—that is, from a language which excludes them from the present, and from man's fears of bringing them over into the present. This is imaged in the thwarted aspirations of trapped birds:

> Flown in from before the cold or nightbound
> (the light attracted them)
>   they sought safety (in books)
> but ended battering against glass
>   at the high windows.

The next reference to the "Beautiful thing" (123:23), itself literally confined between the two halves of a sentence concerning the library's tomblike smell of confining stagnation and death, is connected to the "cost" theme through the phrase "the cost of dreams." By now this cost should be obvious. Dreams become confined in books or in the minds of the men who conceive them; thoughts become confined in the forms and traditions of the past; energy becomes trapped and love becomes enmeshed in systems of pragmatism and use. To maintain any kind of faith in the face of such overwhelming obstacles must indeed place a high price on whatever benefits ultimately may accrue. And Paterson now seems to recognize this:

> Awake, he dozes in a fever heat,
>   cheeks burning   .   .   loaning blood
>   to the past, amazed   .   risking life.

Unlike the dead men whose dreams he is perusing, he is "awake," "dozing" only in the sense that his mind is "reeling, starting back amazed from the reading" (120:30–31). He is in the fever heat of creation, lending life to the past as he recreates its wonder in the present. In so doing, he is necessarily risking his imaginative life: there is always the possibility that his imaginings may fade, forever "joining the others" in the library (or "the sea" of generality which is "not our home"),[3] and that he may become, not what Wallace Stevens has called "the figure of the youth as virile poet,"[4] but an impotent castrate, capable only of "translating." Such an artist has been subjected to "a surgery/ of the wits," for the mind has been cut away, enfeebling forever its creative intent. Paterson averts such a danger, however,

> —and still he brings it back, battering
> with the rest against the vents and high windows
>
> (They do not yield but shriek
> as furies,
> Shriek and execrate the imagination, the impotent
> a woman against a woman, seeking to destroy
> it but it cannot, the life will not out of it).
>
> A library — of books! decrying all books
> that enfeeble the mind's intent
>
> Beautiful thing!

The prose account of the murder of the two Indian braves which now occurs brings together a number of *Paterson's* themes in a rather curious manner. As I have already indicated, on one level the murder is a symbol of the destruction of the local. Like "the last wolf . . . killed near the Weisse Huis in the year 1723," the Indians

---

3. Cf. *Paterson* IV, Section III.
4. See *The Necessary Angel*, pp. 37–68.

were native to the land, and they embodied a principle of natural beauty and energy. On another level the murder is a symbol of the "relentless lust for extermination of the 'bad' savages" of which Williams writes in *In the American Grain* (117)—a symbol of the decidedly "Puritan" attitude which is diametrically opposed to the spirit of communion and love. To Kieft and his acquisitive, pragmatically oriented soldiers, the Indians offered only a threat to the white man's newly gained ascendancy; for the open relation of love they had no "use" whatsoever. "Divorce" from the local, then, which the poem has already presented in particularly aesthetic terms (e.g. the razing of the Castle), is now seen to be at one with divorce from the organic community of one's fellowmen. Finally, of course, the lack of communion is reflected in the lack of a language which is either local to the men of the modern world, or related to that past which it ostensibly describes:

> The Indians were accused of killing two or three pigs—this was untrue, as afterward proved, because the pigs had been butchered by the white men themselves. The following incident is concerned with two of the Indians who had been captured by Kieft's soldiers because of the accusations: The braves had been turned over to the soldiers, by Kieft, to do with as they pleased.

The absence of emotion from this account is striking. Also telling is the fact that concrete particulars, elsewhere one of Williams' poetic ideals, operate here, not to assist love by localizing its objects, but to thwart it by separating feeling from expression: "There stood at the same time, 24 or 25 female savages, who had been taken prisoners, at the north-west corner of the fort: they held up their arms, and in their language exclaimed, 'For shame! for shame! such unheard of cruelty was never known, or even thought of, among us.'" It is significant that only in *their* language is a human response even possible. The various relationships among the members of the primitive community are considered only as sociological phenomena;

the braves' horrible deaths are considered only as historical, or even clinical, events.[5]

The seemingly unrelated passage which follows this prose section is actually a reply to it in the form of serious "wit":

> Doc, listen — fiftyish, a grimy hand
> pushing back the cap: In gold —
> Volunteers of America
>
> I got
> a woman outside I want to marry, will
> you give her a blood test?

The physician here, in contrast to the physician who is Kieft's councilor, is an agent of "marriage," and the "blood test" he will perform, unlike the ordeal witnessed by the Indian women, will further union rather than divorce. To refer again to *In the American Grain:*

> It is *this* to be *moral:* to be *positive,* to be peculiar, to be sure, generous, brave—TO MARRY, to *touch*—to *give* because one HAS, not because one has nothing. And to give to him who HAS, who will join, who will make, who will fertilize, who will be like you yourself: to create, to hybridize, to cross-pollenize, —not to sterilize, to draw back, to fear, to dry up, to rot. [121]

The "gold—/ Volunteers of America" button or insignia is an ironic commentary on both the acquisitiveness and the exploitativeness of Kieft and his men. True riches come only from the local, from the "American." But such freely offered wealth the lust for merely material wealth would only destroy.

Williams' ideals of "marriage" and "energy," however, are not easily attained, and the precariousness of the doctrine affirmed by

5. Cf. the use of the word "fun" here with its use at 65:7.

the poetry at the center of page 126 is indicated by the prose commentary relating to tightrope walking which frames it:

> The place sweats of staleness and of rot
> a back-house stench   .   a
> library stench
>
> It is summer! stinking summer
>
> Escape from it—but not by running
> away. Not by "composition." Embrace the
> foulness
>
> —the being taut, balanced between
> eternities.

Paterson's stream of consciousness has again returned to the library's "foulness." But the vagueness of "The place" and the use of "a/ library stench" as a modifying phrase make the whole section ambiguous: it is impossible to know whether Paterson is in "the streets" or in "the library," for the "stinking summer" from which he is trying to escape (118:1–4) permeates both. But this is just the point. The modern world *is* a library, an imprisoning vault held up only by "useful" systems and authorities. The two worlds are equivalent, or more precisely, the latter is a manifestation and symbol of the former.

Yet escape from either "the world" or "the library" is not to be found in simple withdrawal. The "composition" mentioned here is composition in the traditional forms of the past. These are clearly "stale" themselves and attempt to escape threats simply by ignoring them. A real escape from the confinement of the "stinking summer" comes only through an imaginative transcendence following a recognition that recalcitrance is unescapable. On another level, however, the "it" from which we are to escape may refer, not to a "stinking summer," which symbolizes "The place," but rather to a summer symbolizing the heat of active exuberance. "Escape from it" would then be ironic, related to the "Run from it" passage discussed above, and "summer" would refer specifically to whatever fiery energy is extant in the world. Further, the Whitmanesque phrase, "Embrace the/ foulness," would be the equivalent of the poet's earlier "Blow! . . . Bring down! . . . Consume/ and submerge," "foulness" itself being an ironic comment on the reactions of unimaginative man to the catastrophes.

The poet now gives the "Beautiful thing" a particularly concrete form through the first of two sequences dealing with a girl in a white lace dress. The lyric which begins the section introduces the girl as a wild and natural beauty, apparently the mistress of some local Paterson gang:

> Day is covered and we see you—
>   but not alone!
> drunk and bedraggled to release
>
> the strictness of beauty
> under a sky full of stars
>   Beautiful thing
> and a slow moon—
>   The car
>   had stopped long since
>   when the others
> came and dragged those out
>   who had you there
>   indifferent
> to whatever the anesthetic
>   Beautiful Thing
> might slum away the bars . . .
> —in your white lace dress.

The passage which follows, however, is more crucial. Most important here is the sense of amazement and wonder:

> Haunted, the quietness of your face
> is a quietness, real
>
> out of no book.

Such quietness immediately recalls the quietness associated with
the library and symbolized by the "SILENCE!" sign which Paterson
is presumably sitting in front of (124:8). The silence of the library,
however, is the silence of restraint, passivity, and fear, while the
quietness of the girl's face seems more akin to the quietness at the
center of a maelstrom. The repose she ultimately embodies is not,
that is, the illusory repose to be found in a "book" but rather the
repose of a consummated passion, the repose which is itself the
ultimate manifestation of energy. It is not, as Williams emphasizes,
"easily to be attained."

   Contemplation of the "Beautiful thing" fully revealed would
"purify" the beholder (as well as the "Beautiful thing" itself?),
sending him "hurtling to the moon" in ecstasy. Nonetheless, Paterson is not yet the recipient of such a salvation. I would argue that the
reason for this is to be found in the rigor with which he seeks it:

> Your clothes (I said) quickly, while
> your beauty is attainable.
>
> Put them on the chair
> (I said. Then in a fury, for which I am
> ashamed)
> You smell as though you need
> a bath. Take off your clothes and purify
> yourself   .   .
> And let me purify myself
>
> —to look at you,
> to look at you (I said)
>
> (Then, my anger rising) TAKE OFF YOUR
> CLOTHES!

Beauty is, of course, the stated object of his quest ("Rigor of beauty is the quest. But how will you find beauty when it is locked in the mind past all remonstrance [i.e. showing again]?"). Love and aesthetic apprehension are the keys with which beauty may be released, but both require particular "things" as their objects, and there is an enormous danger that the "quest" will degenerate into a mere desire to appropriate. The protagonist is now "ashamed" of his "fury" (though presumably he was not at the time), and when, in Section II, he does receive the revelation of beauty:

> Later
> Beautiful thing
> I saw you

beauty comes into being through a relationship which is mutual.

With the line, "let's take a ride around, to see what the town looks like," the meaning of the "Beautiful thing" is again broadened, now specifically to include the city. As suggested by *Paterson* III's epigraph, from Santayana's *The Last Puritan* (note title), the city itself should be a manifestation of art and beauty:

> Cities, for Oliver, were not a part of nature. He could hardly feel, he could hardly admit even when it was pointed out to him, that cities are a second body for the human mind, a second organism, more rational, permanent and decorative than the animal organism of flesh and bone: a work of natural yet moral art, where the soul sets up her trophies of action and instruments of pleasure.

But men are indifferent to the city, as they are "indifferent/ to whatever the anesthetic/ Beautiful Thing/ might slum away the bars." They are "Puritans," hostile to "nature" (i.e. the "given") in any of its forms: "So much talk of the language—when there are no/ ears"—which, in the context of Williams' poem, is the same as saying, "so much talk of beauty—when there are no eyes."

Indifference, however, whether to a girl, to a city, or to any other manifestation of beauty, is "the indifference of certain death/ or incident upon certain death." The paradoxical situation of the modern world is simply that while beauty is universally sought, actually it is feared and sought only to be destroyed. This paradox is the riddle of our time—"A marriage riddle":

> What is there to say? save that
> beauty is unheeded   .   tho' for sale and
> bought glibly enough
>
> But it is true, they fear
> it more than death, beauty is feared
> more than death, more than they fear death
>
> Beautiful thing
>
> —and marry only to destroy, in private, in
> their privacy only to destroy, to hide
>   (in marriage)
> that they may destroy and not be perceived
> in it—the destroying.

As I suggested above, the potential cost of beauty is enormous, and men try to bypass this cost, if not through destruction or flight, then through appropriation. But what is bought is, by definition, excluded from Williams' notion of the beautiful. "Marriage" under such conditions—whether between man and woman, or between the artist and the things he sensitively apprehends and creates—is only a mockery of marriage, a rape equivalent to the other modes of destruction appearing throughout the poem. In its solipsistic "privacy" and "hiddenness," such a marriage is ultimately an escape from the exuberant present, being directly related to the escape symbolized by retreat into the library.

The lines which now occur are at once the climax of the section and one of the most moving and significant passages in the poem:

> What end but love, that stares death in the eye?
> A city, a marriage—that stares death
> in the eye
>
> The riddle of a man and a woman
>
> For what is there but love, that stares death
> in the eye, love, begetting marriage—
> not infamy, not death
>
>   tho' love seem to beget
> only death in the old plays, only death, it is
> as tho' they wished death rather than to face
> infamy, the infamy of old cities . . .
>
> Sing me a song to make death tolerable, a song
> of a man and a woman: the riddle of a man
> and a woman.
>   What language could allay our thirsts,
> what winds lift us, what floods bear us
>   past defeats
> but song but deathless song   ?

Love begets marriage and marriage begets life. More precisely, reconciliation with the things of the world (cf. 103:11–12), recognition and acceptance of their value, begets a relationship between man and his world in which he is the recipient of a generous beauty as he is the giver of a generous love. The beauty so attained is the beauty of the eternal present, symbolized by the eternal process of the Falls' sliding waters. It is a beauty which lives forever—transcending the categories of time and mutability because it fearlessly stares the reality of death in the eye. In short, such beauty is the beauty of art, the "enduring" beauty of "the world of imagination" (248:27–29). In the old plays (presumably tragedies) which still hold an iron grip on the present, attempts at "love" did not begin with the local given. Men feared to be reconciled to their world, to embrace the foulness and infamy, and hence could not transcend them. The wasteland of corrupt cities still remains, "nothing else," and because the world is lacking in love, death remains. Indifference, as we have seen, leads to certain death, and indifference is *the* characteristic of acquisitive man. But the thrust of the poem here is toward apocalypse, and the song that will ultimately prevail, the song that will make death tolerable, is the song of "marriage," the deathless song of love.

There now occurs a reminiscence of the voice of the Evangelist of Book II, "clamant/ calling out ceaselessly/ to the birds/ and clouds," while the river of the modern world passes mindlessly by. His is indeed the deathless song of love, and here, as previously, he is intimately related to Paterson himself. But this voice gradually metamorphoses into a new voice, a voice which

> ... rises, neglected
> (with its new) the unfaltering
> language

—the voice of pragmatic objection:

> Give it up. Quit it. Stop writing.
> "Saintlike" you will never
> separate that stain of sense,
>
> an offense
> to love, the mind's worm eating
> out the core, unappeased
>
> —never separate that stain
> of sense from the inert mass. Never.

One may recall Mr. Nixon's advice to the poet of Pound's *Hugh Selwyn Mauberley:*

> "And give up verse, my boy,
> "There's nothing in it."

"Saintlike," especially in this context, seems to be an allusion to Williams' earlier *St. Francis Einstein of the Daffodils* (*CEP* 379–80), a poem which associates Einstein's creative quest for the principle of energy within "the inert mass" of the earth with what Williams elsewhere calls "the thorough logic which St. Francis saw as sparrows or donkeys, equally to be loved with whatever other living aspect of the world."[6]

The voice in *Paterson* goes on to tell the protagonist that he will never succeed in his quest for "that radiance/ quartered apart,/ unapproached by symbols." "That radiance" is "the radiant gist" that figures most importantly in the Madame Curie episode of Book IV. Here, as there, it is associated with love, beauty, and energy. Particularly important are the parallels Williams eventually draws among the poet (or Paterson), Madame Curie, and Columbus. The life goal of each is a discovery: for Madame Curie, the discovery of radium, "the radiant gist . . . in the pitch-blend" (133:6–9); for Columbus, "The Discovery of the Indies" (*Grain* 7), "The New World, existing in those times beyond the sphere of all things known to history, [lying] . . . as the middle of the desert or the sea lies now and must lie forever, marked with its own dark life in which we have no part" (*Grain* 7); for the poet, the discovery of that "beauty" which "is locked in the mind past all remonstrance." In each case, however, failure and disillusionment threaten the quester at every turn. The woman physicist toils "with coarsened hands/ by the hour, the day, the week/ to get, after months of labor   ./ a stain at the bottom of the retort/ without weight, a failure, a/ nothing" (209:1–6). The explorer suffers "boundless grief and trouble"

6. Quoted by Brinnin, *William Carlos Williams,* pp. 20–21.

(*Grain* 8), continuing "voyage after voyage, four times, out of his
growing despair" (*Grain* 11), until he can say only, "Such is my
fate, that the twenty years of service through which I have passed
with so much toil and danger, have profited me nothing" (*Grain* 14).
As for the poet, he is told to

> Give up
> the poem. Give up the shilly-
> shally of art.

> What can you, what
> can YOU hope to conclude--
> on a heap of dirty linen?

> —you
> a poet (ridded) from Paradise?

and, as the voice continues its taunting:

> Death lies in wait
> a kindly brother—
> full of the missing words,
> the words that never get said—
> a kindly brother to the poor.

But apparent failure and disillusionment are ultimately irrelevant.
Madame Curie, "returning in the/ night" to the laboratory, observes
the stain "to find it LUMINOUS!" (209:6–8). Columbus, anchoring
in the New World "On Friday, the twelfth of October," walks
"among the trees which was the most beautiful thing which [he]
had ever known" (209:9–14).[7] And the poet, if only momentarily,
will find the "Beautiful thing." Williams, then, has created a "myth"
—a myth which permits the emphasis, even the celebration, of

7. The corresponding passage in *In the American Grain* is to be found
on page 26. It might be noted that Williams has slightly modified this sentence in *Paterson* by changing "seen" to "known" (i.e. "realize").

recalcitrance and apparent failure, because the degree of such frustration is paradoxically a measure of ultimate fulfillment. Williams writes in the letter to Horace Gregory (July 22, 1939) that the Columbus essay in *In the American Grain* was very carefully designed to embody this myth: "I wrote and rewrote that ten times before I got hold of the idea which I finally adopted. The problem was to include all the four voyages and yet make the essay end on the high point of the successful termination of the first voyage with the tremendous emotional power centered there."[8] Its embodiment in both the form and content of "the impossible poem *Paterson*" (*SL* 230) is more complex, but Williams' epic does, I think, bring the earlier analogue to its logical end.

The challenge continues, emphasizing the "cost" and "uselessness" of the artist's dream and suggesting that only "a dirty book" is capable of bringing the artist any practical returns. The voice also objects to Paterson/Williams' belief in "the People," Hamilton's "great beast":

> Doctor, do you believe in
> "the people," the Democracy? Do
> you still believe — in this
> swill-hole of corrupt cities?
> Do you, Doctor? Now?

But as the sequence discussed above insists, even in this "world of corrupt cities" (cf. 130:18) the faith in man that is a form of love is "still" possible (in addition to its modern meaning, the adverb also carries its older force of "always").

As Section I draws to a close, then, a more positive voice presses toward an ultimate affirmation of energy:

> Try another book. Break through
> the dry air of the place

and:

---

8. *Selected Letters*, p. 185. Cf. *I Wanted To Write a Poem*, p. 42.

> Quit it. Quit this place. Go where all
> mouths are rinsed: to the river for
> an answer
>   for relief from "meaning"

"A tornado approaches," perhaps emphasizing in its uniqueness ("We don't have/ tornados in these latitudes. What, at/ Cherry Hill?") the singularity of the poet's position.

>   It pours
>   over the roofs of Paterson, ripping,
>   twisting, tortuous.

As a symbol of release and exuberance, the tornado is related to the overtly sexual energies described in the passage just before:

> An insane god
>   —nights in a brothel
>   And if I had   .
> What then?
>
>   —made brothels my home?
>   (Toulouse Lautrec
>   again.   .   )

Toulouse-Lautrec is noted for his peculiarly twentieth-century insistence upon the right of the artist to choose his material, irrespective of traditional associations of "beauty" or "goodness." Such a position is basic to the poetry of William Carlos Williams. As he put it in the Mike Wallace interview, a part of which is printed in *Paterson* V (dedicated, significantly, "To the Memory of HENRI TOULOUSE LAUTREC, *Painter*"), "Anything is good material for poetry. Anything. I've said it time and time again" (262:16–17). The point is not, of course, that sordidness in art is somehow a virtue in itself, but simply that the prosaic connotations of the artistic subject are irrelevant. If a sense of "life," which will ultimately both assimilate and transcend the traditional associations, can be discovered, that and that only is of any concern to art. At one imaginative extreme, then, "The whore and the virgin" are "an identity" (245:14).[9]

Something like this seems to be involved in the rather curious passage which follows:

> Say I am the locus
>> where two women meet
>
> One from the backwoods
>> a touch of the savage
>> and of T.B.
>> (a scar on the thigh)
> The other   —   wanting,
>> from an old culture   .
> —and offer the same dish
>> different ways.

The first woman seems to be the gang mistress of Section II: the "scar on/ the thigh" is specifically emphasized when the protagonist finally "sees" the "Beautiful Thing" in the basement ("You showed me your legs, scarred (as a child)/ by the whip"—152:1–2).[10] The

9. When Williams writes this, he also means that the virgin "who does not give herself to her lover/ —forthwith" (266:23–24) is equivalent to (in the sense that she is "no better than") the common prostitute our Urizenic society so hypocritically condemns: "The moral/ proclaimed by the whorehouse/ could not be better proclaimed/ by the virgin, a price on her head,/ her maidenhead!/ sharp practice/ to hold on to that/ cheapening it:/ Throw it away!" (242:24–243:6). But, especially in the context of *Paterson* V, the more positive interpretation is most important. Cf. Williams' statement, in a conversation with John C. Thirlwall, "William Carlos Williams' *Paterson*," p. 258: "I've always had the idea that whore is right. Sex is the only way of liberation of woman from man."

10. Cf. 146:15.

second woman is "from an old culture"—not, apparently, the primitive culture of the "Indians" (which is associated with openness and fertility), but rather the "old-fashioned" culture of the "Puritans." She is only "from" such a culture, however, not "of" it, and if she wants (i.e. lacks) experience, she presumably desires and needs it as well. The two women "offer the same dish," then, not only in the simply sexual sense, but also—and this is what is finally important—in the aesthetic sense. Both being associated with exuberance and generosity, they both provide positive content for an art which simultaneously assimilates them ("Say I am the locus/ where two women meet") and transcends them ("the virgin and the whore, which/ most endures? the world/ of the imagination most endures" —248:27–29). To such an art, and to the eternal energy it embodies, the poet gives himself in "wonder" ("a wooden shingle driven half its length/ into an oak . . . The church/ moved 8 inches through an arc, on its/ foundations"). At the section's conclusion he is still "Searching among books"—"Seeking"—but his "mind" is "elsewhere." "Looking down" upon the river running to the sea below the Falls, he may perhaps be "confused," as was Sam Patch before his fatal leap. But he knows his place is ultimately in the eternally suspended "catastrophe of the descent"—itself, of course, associated with the humming wind.

TOUCHED BY THE FIRE

Section II begins with a passage of considerable irony and complexity:

> Fire burns; that is the first law.
> When a wind fans it the flames
>
> are carried abroad. Talk
> fans the flames.

To unimaginative men fire poses only a threat: it destroys what they might otherwise acquire or use. Preservation of self and property is, of course, the foundation of our whole legal system, and as fear of fire is impressed upon the child, so is fear of material destruction instilled into the man. To imaginative men, however, burning by fire carries the same ambiguities as drowning by water. In each case the "destruction" may be "creative," associated with purification and rebirth. And as we have already seen, fire is also a symbol of the energy inseparable from "Beautiful things." The poet, then, sees the spreading of flames by the wind (itself a symbol of imaginative energy) as a symbolically positive good—indicative that imagination and positive relationship (the "approach" suggested by "Talk") are spreading among mankind.

The next few lines of the sequence deal specifically with contrasting attitudes toward "writing":

> ... They have
>
> manoeuvred it so that to write
> is a fire and not only of the blood.
>
> The writing is nothing, the being
> in a position to write (that's
>
> where they get you) is nine tenths
> of the difficulty: seduction
>
> or strong arm stuff. The writing
> should be a relief,
>
> relief from the conditions
> which as we advance become — a fire,
>
> a destroying fire. For the writing
> is also an attack and means must be
>
> found to scotch it — at the root
> if possible. So that

> to write, nine tenths of the problem
> is to live.

The "they" here is the same amorphous mass of unimaginative men that "broke" the union-opposing Lambert. To "them" writing is an awesome and threatening "fire," not only of the blood but presumably of the mind as well. The rational faculty, that is to say, is "menaced" by the visionary faculty—by "The Dangerous Prevalence of Imagination." That these lines are to be taken as ironic, even grimly humorous, is suggested, I think, through a tone of self-induced fear and awe, a tone particularly emphasized by the mechanicalness of the word "manoeuvred." To such minds neither the product nor the process of writing is as significant as "the being in a position to write." On one level, of course, this latter phrase may refer to the accomplishments and conditions conventionally assumed requisite for a writer (time, livelihood, skill, knowledge of poetic tradition and technique). On another level, however, "being in a position to write" may refer to the fiery impulse which seems to compel imaginative man to create. Read in this way, the lines are involved with an ostensible threat to the poet's sanity. Presumably, writing should be a "relief," not only an "escape" from "foulness" and "infamy,"[11] but also a kind of psychic and aesthetic "release" from destroying "madness." But the writing is itself an outburst of energy, and means must finally be found to stifle it, even as means must finally be found to stifle the destroying fire behind it. The "to live" at the end of this quotation may mean "to have the means to live," but it may also mean "to preserve oneself from the devouring fire."

Upon all these meanings, however, are superimposed their contraries as seen by the creative and imaginative poet. Writing does involve a fire, and a fire not only of the blood; but such a fire is certainly not to be feared. The difficulty for the poet to become identified with it is, of course, one of the central themes of the poem.

11. Cf. Williams' treatment of "composition" at 126:18–20.

On the one hand, the poet must really fight against the pressures of everyday reality (in another context, Williams even writes, "I plan one thing—that I could press/ buttons to do the curing of or caring for/ the sick that I do laboriously now by hand/ for cash, to have the time/ when I am fresh, in the morning, when/ my mind is clear and burning—to write"—*CEP* 238). On the other hand, the attainment of the fiery imaginative impulse really does involve an enormous effort. It is ironically a fact, therefore, that both "living" and "imaginative living" are indeed nine-tenths of the problem of writing.

The sequence concludes with a series of quotations illustrating unimaginative ("sub-intellectual") blindness even further:

> . . . We're so proud of you!
>
> A wonderful gift! How *do*
> you fiind the time for it in
>
> your busy life? It must be a great
> thing to have such a pastime.
>
> But you were always a strange
> boy. How's your mother?

The force of "wonderful" here is almost tragic. Even when the quester's quest is at last completed, the unanswerable objection will remain:

> —the cyclonic fury, the fire,
> the leaden flood and finally
> the cost—
>
> Your father was *such* a nice man.
> I remember him well   .
>
> Or, Geeze, Doc, I guess it's all right
> but what the hell does it mean?

Somewhat more than six years after these lines were written, Williams had this to say about the problems they involve:

> When the world asks: "Gee, doc, what does it all mean?" they respect me, not as a doctor, but because of this world which they don't understand—an elevated world which they know exists and which they would see manifested in me—a world which scares them because it is above them. . . . I have always tried to lead an elevated life, which they respect even if they don't share it.[12]

Ultimately, of course, such comments as these are very much in the spirit of *Paterson* as a whole. In the passage I have been discussing, however, admittedly a part of the most "apocalyptic" book of the poem, Williams' toleration for the unimaginative seems considerably less.

The themes of ignorance and restraint are continued in the prose episode which follows. Appropriately enough, since the section precedes that concerning a fire, the central symbol is smoke. The smoke, however, is a substitute for, and not a product of, the fire; it is in fact produced by the *extinguishing* of a fire that is barely beginning to smolder:

> With due ceremony a hut would be constructed consisting of twelve poles, each of a different species of wood. These they run into the ground, tie them together at the top, cover them entirely with bark, skins or blankets joined close together.
> .   Now here is where one sits who will address the Spirit of Fire, He-Who-Lies-With-His-Eyes-Bulging-In-The-Smoke-Hole   .   Twelve *manittos* attend him as subordinate deities, half representing animals and the others vegetables. A large oven is built in the house of sacrifice   .   heated with twelve large red-hot stones.

12. Quoted by Thirlwall, p. 277.

Meanwhile an old man throws twelve pipefuls of tobacco upon the hot stones, and directly another follows and pours water on them, which occasions a smoke or vapor almost powerful enough to suffocate the persons in the tent —

Those sitting in the tent have come to address only "the *Spirit* of Fire" (italics mine). The "tepee" is therefore identified with the "library," for just as men seek sanctuary in the latter because they know they will find only "a wind or ghost of a wind" echoing life, so men seek sanctuary in the former because they know they will find only "smoke." The smoke is suffocating, but "He-Who-Lies-With-His-Eyes-Bulging-In-The-Smoke-Hole" is incapable of recognizing this.

Paterson, however, "breathing the books in," clearly realizes that he is inhaling only "acrid fumes," and that he is receiving nothing more than what even unimaginative men could "decipher" themselves. He is "warping" his mind (the phrase "warping the sense" also refers to unimaginative modes of reading and writing) merely to "detect the norm," and instead of breaking through the bonds of conventional restraint (134:1), he is only confining himself further to its fearful evasions of "affection, women and offspring."

The fire starts "in the car barns of the street railway company, in the paint shop," and

> Breathless and in haste
> the various night (of books) awakes! awakes
> and begins (a second time) its song, pending the
> obloquy of dawn   .

The library, one might recall, "eased" the "breathlessness" with which one escaped into its sanctuary (120:15–17). Here, however, the breathlessness arises not in escape *from* energy but in escape *of* energy; sleeping men and ideas awaken and resume the exuberant songs previously stifled by the confinements of language, convention, and pragmatism. "Night" here is associated with the deathlike sleep of books, but in its "awakened" form it is associated with ultimate (poetic) consciousness. The "obloquy of dawn" is both the wind which spreads the fire at dawn and an ironic reference to the censure of "common" day. The brief reference to the cyclotron ("A cyclotron, a "sifting"") thus recalls the theme of the "radiant gist." Like the fire, the cyclotron destroys to create ("a dispersal and a metamorphosis"). Equally important, the cyclotron has the capacity to energize, to "excite" or "awaken" whatever is subjected to its forces.

Nonetheless, most men are in a druglike sleep:

> And there,
> in the tobacco hush : in a tepee they lie
> huddled (a huddle of books)
> > antagonistic,
> > > and dream of
> gentleness—under the malignity of the hush
> they cannot penetrate and cannot waken, to be again
> active but remain—books
> > that is, men in hell,
> their reign over the living ended.

The tobacco hush here is the same as the books' silence. Out of fear we huddle together in a tent of our own creation, our imaginative and energetic capacity entombed as within a book. We are antagonistic to these qualities as we are "hidden from/ affection, women and offspring." We dream only of gentleness, of the cool havens in which we may hide from our fears. And under the malignity of the hush of a deathly, uncreative silence we choose to remain—in a hell of our own making, utterly cut off from the life of creation, imagination, and love. The lines which conclude this sequence are to me profoundly moving. We live in a world in which the "value" of everything is "clearly" marked, a world in which everything is "clearly" understood:

Clearly, they say. Oh clearly! Clearly?
What more clear than that of all things
nothing is so unclear, between man and
his writing, as to which is the man and
which the thing and of them both which
is the more to be valued.[13]

These are the words of despair—but of a prophetic despair, of
a despair that heralds apocalypse. The fire, fanned by the dawn
wind, is soon raging "out of control—sweeping the block and
heading toward the business district." There may be a sexual implication here. At any rate, the "Beautiful thing" is now reinvoked
in all its complexity:

Beautiful thing
              —the whole city doomed! And
    the flames towering   .

The "destruction" of the city is "beautiful" both in itself, as a
"wonder" and as a manifestation of energy, and through its effects,
as creative destroyer.[14] The creative destruction is suggested
through the mutual nourishment Paterson and the flame paradoxically provide one another:

The night was made day by the flames, flames
on which he fed—grubbing the page
                          (the burning page)
like a worm—for enlightenment

13. Cf. *Paterson* I, 31:17-19: "Clearly!/ speaks the red-breast his behest.
Clearly!/ clearly!"
14. In *In the American Grain,* "The Destruction of Tenochtitlan" (27-38)
is not such a creative destruction. Cortez, ultimately, is a "Puritan," and the
conclusion of the chapter—"Later the Conqueror *tried* to rebuild the city"
(italics mine)—is ironic.

> Of which we drink and are drunk and in the end
> are destroyed (as we feed). But the flames
> are flames with a requirement, a belly of their
> own that destroys.

One need only note the important distinction emphasized by the first parenthetical expression. Drunkenness and destructiveness have, of course, already been associated with the "Beautiful thing."

A brief allusion to "fires that/ smolder/ smolder a lifetime and never burst/ into flame"—fires already introduced in relation to the "Spirit of Fire"—leads to one of the section's most important statements. "An old bottle mauled" (introduced 191:16–17) survives the apocalyptic conflagration, as an artifact of fiery creativity:

> A bottle, mauled
> by the flames, belly-bent with laughter:
> yellow, green. So be it—of drunkenness
> survived, in guffaws of flame.

The original bottle itself has ceased to exist; an entirely new creation ("an old bottle mauled") has come into being:

> So be it. The beauty of fire-blasted sand
> that was glass, that was a bottle: unbottled.
> unabashed. So be it.
>
> An old bottle, mauled by the fire
> gets a new glaze, the glass warped
> to a new distinction, reclaiming the
> undefined.

One should note the effectiveness of Williams' use of excessive laughter in this episode to suggest both the exuberance and the terror of the creative/destructive energy with which he is concerned. The image "belly-bent with laughter" is both an accurate description of how a mauled bottle may look and a means of giving it virtually human status. Most important of all are the lines:

>   . . . The glass
> splotched with concentric rainbows
> of cold fire that the fire has bequeathed
> there as it cools, its flame
> defied—the flame that wrapped the glass
> deflowered, reflowered there by
> the flame: a second flame, surpassing
> heat   .

The flame surpassing heat is the flame which comes into being when, and only when, the supremely sensitive mind imaginatively apprehends the objective "thing" before it. The mauled bottle, like any work of art, may not be appreciated *as* art, even though it is "created" as art by the artist. But if the beholder, through his own imaginative effort, is able to "see" the concentric rainbows of cold fire that the artist's flame has bequeathed, his imagination becomes one with the imagination of the artist. Imaginative apprehension is therefore the means by which art and "the world of the imagination" endure, even after the creative flame has disappeared—the means by which the "poet" (i.e. any imaginative apprehender) is able to beat the initial fire at its own game:

>   . . . Beat you
> at your own game, Fire. Outlast you:
> Poet Beats Fire at Its Own Game! The bottle!
> the bottle! the bottle! the bottle! *I*
> give *you* the bottle! What's burning
> now, Fire?   [italics mine]

Now the poet again refers to the spectacle of the burning library as a "Beautiful thing," this time specifically because it involves a defiance of authority (one may recall the defiance of Lambert in Section I):

> a defiance of authority
> —burnt Sappho's poems, burned
> by intention (or are they still hid
> in the Vatican crypts?)   :
>
> beauty is
> a defiance of authority

The "perfection" associated with Sappho's poems ("She avoided all roughness"—253:2–3) is then contrasted with the "vulgarity of beauty" to be found in the here and now:

> Beautiful thing, your
> vulgarity of beauty surpasses all their
> perfections!
> Vulgarity surpasses all perfections
> —it leaps from a varnish pot and we see
> it pass—in flames!

Williams does not, of course, reject either the elegance of form or the elevation of content associated with Sapphic verse. Indeed, if he is "no authority on Sappho" and does "not read her poetry particularly well" (235:1–2), his "modern" translation, which is placed at the beginning of the second section of *Paterson* V, is remarkably effective.[15] It is important to recognize, however, that Williams is concerned with Sappho's poems only because he considers them to be timeless and contemporary: "My purpose was to speak as I thought this remarkable woman meant to speak—not what the classic English students had done to her in their stilted translations. I had the poem read aloud to me, over and over, in the original Greek by scholars who knew how the words should sound so that I might catch the rise and fall of the beat."[16] Williams' "translation," although stylized, utilizes contemporary American rhythms, more or

15. This translation was published separately in *Poems in Folio* (San Francisco, 1957).

16. *I Wanted To Write a Poem*, pp. 92–93.

less normal word order, and surprisingly idiomatic language. In one sense, that is, he has "burned" Sappho's poems by the very process of writing them anew—rekindling them and, as it were, recovering them from the dead:

> for they were
> unwrapped, fragment by fragment, from
> outer mummy cases of papier mâché inside
> Egyptian sarcophagi   .
>
>   flying papers
> from old conflagrations, picked up
> haphazard by the undertakers to make
> moulds, layer after layer
>   for the dead
> Beautiful thing.[17]

17. Cf. the following passage from Williams' essay "Against the Weather: A Study of the Artist," first published in 1939, ten years before the publication of *Paterson* III: "The extreme example of the principle of sabotage as practiced by parties upon the arts was the destruction of the library at Alexandria. So valuable was the work of the artist there that to this day we unglue the backs of old books and even pick apart the lids of sarcophagi in order to find perhaps one line of Sappho" (*Selected Essays of William Carlos Williams* [New York, Random House, 1954], p. 199). This passage does not, of course, really contradict his statements in *Paterson,* as my discussion should make clear. In a very different context, Harold Bloom (in "Keats and the Embarrassments of Poetic Tradition," in *From Sensibility to Romanticism,* ed. Frederick W. Hilles and Harold Bloom [New York, Oxford University Press, 1965], p. 513) has described the paradox involved as follows:

One of the central themes in W. J. Bate's definitive *John Keats* is the "large, often paralyzing embarrassment . . . that the rich accumulation of past poetry, as the eighteenth century had seen so realistically, can curse as well as bless." As Mr. Bate remarks, this embarrassment haunted Romantic and haunts post-Romantic poetry, and was felt by Keats with a particular intensity. Somewhere in the heart of each new poet there is hidden the dark wish that the libraries be burned in some new Alexandrian conflagration, that the imagination might be liberated from the greatness and oppressive power of its own dead champions.

To a large extent, then Sappho's poems are indistinguishable from Williams' more habitual kind of poetry; or, to put it even more accurately, Williams' habitual kind of poetry is essentially an expression of the most enduring qualities of Sappho's. This point is supported by the fact that the poem beginning "There is a woman in our town" (in V, ii) is written as a formal parallel to Sappho's "Peer of the gods."[18] As we have already seen, beauty is inseparable from exuberance: as "the flame's lover" (148:16–17) the "Beautiful thing" is "intertwined with the fire." From such an "identity" we shrink, "squirting little hoses of/ objection," Paterson/Williams "along with the rest, squirting/ at the fire," for we fear beauty even more than death:

> . . . (we die in silence, we
> enjoy shamefacedly—in silence, hiding
> our joy even from each other
> > keeping
> a secret joy in the flame which we dare
> not acknowledge).

With the description of the floating roof the section rises to another major climax:

> a shriek of fire with
> the upwind, whirling the room away—to reveal
> the awesome sight of a tin roof (1880)
> entire, half a block long, lifted like a
> skirt, held by the fire—to rise at last,
> almost with a sigh, rise and float, float
> upon the flames as upon a sweet breeze,
> and majestically drift off, riding the air,

18. The two poems are similar in verse form (especially in *not* being triadic) as well as in content. Together they function as a kind of frame for the letter from Pound, judging it. To stress differences between the two is to miss the whole point of the sequence.

            sliding
    upon the air, easily and away over
    the frizzled elms that seem to bend under
    it, clearing the railroad tracks to fall
    upon the roofs beyond, red hot
    darkening the rooms
                    (but not our minds).

The key word here is "awesome," for like the city of Tenochtitlan in
In the American Grain (30), and like the tornado in Section I, the
phenomenon described here is a "wonder." In its awesome combina-
tion of terror and beauty, it is clearly another manifestation of the
"Beautiful thing," and ultimately, through such words as "float" and
"sliding,"[19] it is related to the central "wonder" of the poem, the
Passaic Falls. Consequently,

        . . . we stand with our mouths open,
        shaking our heads and saying, My God, did
        you ever see anything like that? As though
        it were wholly out of our dreams, as
        indeed it is, unparalleled in our most sanguine
        dreams   .

In lines 140:9–18 the poet had spoken despairingly of our "dream[s]
of gentleness—under the malignity of the hush/ they cannot pene-
trate." Marvels may occur, however, beyond even our most violent
dreams—accompanied, moreover, not by silence, but by "a roar"
and "an outcry/ which none can afford." While we stand apprehend-
ing such spectacles in amazement, "submerged in wonder," we enter
an imaginative union with them, as "the person/ passed into the
flames, becomes the flames—/ the flame taking over the person . . .
the fire become the person." Such a union is another "marriage"
begotten by "love."

   19. Cf. esp. 16:18–22, 19:15, and 173:7.

In contrast to this rare wonder Williams once more juxtaposes the sterile values of the library:

> That which should be
> rare is trash; because it contains
> nothing of you. They spit on you,
> literally, but without you, nothing. The
> library is muffled and dead
>
> But you are the dream
> of dead men
>
> Beautiful thing!

"Dream" here recalls the whole complex of meanings thus far developed in the poem, referring to the dreams which are confined by the walls of language or repression (cf. 123:10) to the dreams of passivity and gentleness (cf. 140:13–14), and to the more exuberant dreams the "costs" of which are so enormous (cf. 124:1, 146:22–23, 147:22–25). The tin roof "wonder" is attended by a "roar," an "outcry," and a "shriek of fire." The library, however, is muffled and silent. And because it is silent, it "must go down":

> BECAUSE IT IS SILENT. IT
> IS SILENT BY DEFECT OF VIRTUE IN THAT IT
> CONTAINS NOTHING OF YOU.

The remainder of Section II deals with Paterson's second vision of the girl in the white lace dress. The episode itself is introduced by an extraordinary letter from someone called "DJB" to his "Hon." In contrast to the "white hot man become/ a book" whom Williams describes just before, "DJB" is a symbol for the energetic man whose "new way of talking" and writing is as alive as his sensibilities:

Hi Kid
   I know you just about to shot me. But honest Hon. I have really been to busy to write. Here there, and everywhere.
   Bab I haven't wrote since October so I will go back to Oct.

31, (Oh by the way are friend Madam B. Harris had a party the
31, but only high browns and *yellow* so I wasn't invited)
    But I pay that no mind, cause I really (pitched myself a ball)
Went to the show early in the day, and then to the dance at the
club. had me a (some kinded fine time) I was feeling good believe me you. child. . . .

Like the lyric which introduces the first "Beautiful Thing" sequence,
most of the subjects of this letter are overtly sexual, and it consequently provides an appropriate transition to the "Beautiful
Thing" passage which follows. As on the earlier occasion, however,
Williams is concerned with the sexual only as it relates to his over-
all theme. The vision comes somewhat unexpectedly, being announced only by the simple lines,

> Later
> > Beautiful thing

> > > I saw you.

The reference to the "Lady of the House" is somewhat ambiguous.
Of course, we may assume that she is simply the landlady of some
squalid rooming establishment, but it is also possible that she is
the madam of the brothel mentioned earlier (134:3–9, 245:14–15).
This seems particularly suggested by the fact that her title is
capitalized. At any rate, Paterson finds the girl "stretched out negli-
gently on the dirty sheet," "by the laundry tubs" in the basement—
these details, together with the fact that Paterson's eye is at the "level
of the ground," recalling the theme of the "descent."[20] Presumably
her body is now revealed, and its beauty makes the entire scene
"holy." Paterson's response is one of awesome wonder:

20. The phrase "Persephone gone to hell" is almost certainly related to
the title of Williams' unique book *Kora in Hell: Improvisations* (Boston,
1920; see *I Wanted To Write a Poem*, pp. 26–31).

                              —for I was overcome
            by amazement and could do nothing but admire
            and lean to care for you in your quietness.

Such a response is the approach of nonappropriating relationship,
the love of beauty as a fulfilling end in itself. It is a mutual relationship, for beauty is dependent upon love. As the "mauled bottle"
passage exemplifies such mutuality in man's relation to art, so this
episode exemplifies it in man's relation to other human beings:

            [You] looked at me, smiling and we remained
            thus looking, each at the other   .   in silence   .

            You lethargic, waiting upon me, waiting for
            the fire and I
                  attendant upon you, shaken by your beauty

            Shaken by your beauty   .
                              Shaken.

The "silence" and "quietness" here I have already discussed in regard
to earlier episodes; and the thrice-repeated "shaken" relates the
passage even closer to the symbolic meanings of the Falls.
   Paterson is now shown the girl's scarred legs, "scarred (as a child)/
by the whip." Shortly after, we learn something further about the
"Beautiful Thing's" history:

                  And the guys from Paterson . . .
                  socked you one
                        across the nose
                        Beautiful Thing
                  for good luck and emphasis
                        cracking it
                  till I must believe that all

desired women have had each
in the end
a busted nose
and live afterward marked up
Beautiful Thing
for memory's sake
to be credible in their deeds

Monroe K. Spears[21] has written that this passage is totally incomprehensible to him. In terms of the symbolic structure of Williams' poem, however, it seems to refer both to the destructive energy which is the necessary concomitant of the beautiful, and to Williams' belief that the potential "vulgarity" of such energy is irrelevant. As Yeats puts it in the well-known conclusion to *Crazy Jane Talks with the Bishop:*

> . . . nothing can be sole or whole
> That has not been rent.

Embedded, appropriately enough, in the middle of the description of the "Beautiful Thing's" being whipped (152:2) and "maled/ and femaled" (153:28–29), there occurs a brief sequence concerning the active imaginative effort which man must make if he is to discover that energetic beauty which is the peculiar characteristic of such events:

> Read. Bring the mind back (attendant upon
> the page) to the day's heat. The page also is
> the same beauty : a dry beauty of the page—
> beaten by whips

21. "The Failure of Language," *Poetry,* 76 (1950), 39–44. It should be noted that the lines in question are part of the conclusion to the longish lyric Williams originally published as *Paterson: Episode 17* (*CEP* 438–42). The bulk of this poem has been worked into the present *Paterson* III, but only in bits and snatches.

> A tapestry hound
> with his thread teeth drawing crimson from
> the throat of the unicorn.

The full apprehension of a tapestry,[22] of the written page (whether prose or poetry, old or new), or of one's beloved—or, more generally, the full apprehension of the "Beautiful Things" of both art and life—all involve the same imaginative process on the part of both artist and audience. Section II concludes, then, with a brief but very moving statement of the poet's faith in the power of love:

> I can't be half gentle enough,
> half tender enough
> toward you, toward you,
> inarticulate, not half loving enough
>
> BRIGHTen
> the cor
>   ner
> where you are
>   —a flame,
> black plush, a dark flame.

The "dark flame" has previously referred both to the many suggestions of "fire" and to the colored girl who is the "Beautiful Thing" (123:7–8). Gentleness and tenderness "toward" something external to the self, whether another human being or an object of human or natural art, is the loving approach which culminates in "marriage."

22. This is, of course, a reference to the famous Unicorn Tapestries now at the Cloisters in New York, specifically to a detail of the extraordinary sixth tapestry. As Martz has shown ("The Unicorn in *Paterson*," pp. 537–54), these tapestries figure as a crucial symbol in *Paterson* V, emphasizing the importance of the details out of which the larger fabric of the work of art can ultimately be woven. Here in *Paterson* III, however, the significance of the reference is primarily in its more obvious content.

Through the mutuality of the relationship involved, man brightens as he is himself brightened, receiving as well as bestowing the dark flame of imagination and love. The joy of such a marriage is quietly but powerfully suggested by the almost musical notation of the phrase from Rodeheaver's once-popular tune.

BESIDE THE SLIDING WATER

Like Section I, Section III begins with an interior dialogue between two antithetical voices. Here, however, the voice opposing the poet is presented with an irony as intense as the irony accompanying the voice at the beginning of Section II: it in no way poses threats that the poet must "overcome" or even seriously consider:

> It is dangerous to leave written that which is badly written. A chance word, upon paper, may destroy the world. Watch carefully and erase, while the power is still yours, I say to myself, for all that is put down, once it escapes, may rot its way into a thousand minds, the corn become a black smut, and all libraries, of necessity, be burned to the ground as a consequence.

> Only one answer: write carelessly so that nothing that is not green will survive.

Needless to say, this is not an apologia for slovenliness. Rather, it is a forceful plea for imagination, energy, and spontaneity—for a kind of writing the "truth" of which lies beyond stylistic nicety, logical consistency, and even moral and social conventionality. Such writing, to the man of confined imagination, is "bad," both in itself and in its effects. In reality, of course, it is a manifestation of beauty, but because its potential disruptiveness is feared, it must be suppressed. Should imaginative energy still somehow "escape" and "rot" all thought, to preserve "order" and "sanity," the libraries, in an ironic parody of the imaginative conflagration affirmed in the section just before, would have to be burned.

Following this introduction there occurs a strange, nightmarish lyric introducing the flood imagery which dominates Section III as wind and fire imagery dominates Sections I and II:

> There is a drumming of submerged
> engines, a beat of propellers.
> The ears are water. The feet
> listen. Boney fish bearing lights
> stalk the eyes—which float about,
> indifferent. A taste of iodine
> stagnates upon the law of percent-
> ages: thick boards bored through
> by worms whose calcined husks
> cut our fingers, which bleed   .

The "drumming of submerged/ engines" and "beat of propellers" are undoubtedly to be associated with the sounds of modern civilization. Our world is "submerged" beneath a "flood" in the same way that it is "entombed" within a "library." The "Boney fish bearing lights . . . which float about,/ indifferent" are therefore the horrible representations of the modern human beings whose "indifference" we have already seen to be the indifference of death-in-life. They "bear" light only in the sense that they carry it (as a burden)—they cannot create it—and indeed, the very darkness in which they wander is less a manifestation of reality than it is a manifestation of their own unimaginative self-constraint. The skeletal forms which suggest their sterile and stagnant imaginations continually mock ("stalk the eyes of") the more imaginative protagonist.

The relationship between flood and library seems also to be indicated by the rather fragmentary lines,

> We walk into a dream, from certainty to the unascertained,
> in time to see   .   from the roseate past   .   a
> ribbed tail deploying

The "dream" involved here is not the dream of a true poet, for such a man securely grounds his imaginative vision in a spatially and temporally local reality. On the contrary, it is simply the dream of the unimaginative escapist, the man who flees the certainties of the local to seek an illusory sanctuary in the "roseate past." As Paterson has learned, however, such a seeker will find only the roar of a deafening oppressiveness.

This roar, as we would expect, now becomes associated with the flood, but before the association is made explicit, the flood symbol itself is presented in more general terms:

> Upon which there intervenes
> a sour stench of embers. So be it. Rain
> falls and surfeits the river's upper reaches,
> gathering slowly. So be it. Draws together,
> runnel by runnel. . . .
> . . . Men stand at the bridge, silent,
> watching. So be it. So be it.

The "sour stench of embers" is the odor of the fire extinguished by the flood. The image, on one level at least, suggests the extinguishing of energy that Williams sees as the perennial fate of ideas, cultures, and individual men. Here, as previously, the use of the "So be it" formula clearly indicates the reconstructive aspects of the catastrophe, but again such aspects are neither understood nor appreciated by the unimaginative men who witness it.

All these themes come together in the important verse paragraph which follows:

> And there rises
> a counterpart, of reading, slowly, overwhelming
> the mind; anchors him in his chair. So be
> it. He turns   .   O Paradiso! The stream
> grows leaden within him, his lilies drag. So
> be it. Texts mount and complicate them-
> selves, lead to further texts and those
> to synopses, digests and emendations. So be it.
> Until the words break loose or—sadly

>hold, unshaken. Unshaken! So be it. For
>the made-arch holds, the water piles up debris
>against it but it is unshaken. They gather
>upon the bridge and look down, unshaken.
>So be it. So be it. So be it.

Mainly, of course, that which surfeits the upper reaches of the mind's stream of thought is simply academicism. Paterson, unlike the lilies of lines 11–13, which make a desperate attempt to remain above the rising waters, surrenders to the flood, or, in terms of the parallel symbols, allows himself to be anchored all the more firmly to his chair in the library. As the radiant gist of uranium gradually loses energy to become lead within the pitchblende that contains it, so the stream of Paterson's consciousness grows leaden within him. Presumably, such a clogging of the mind should continue only until the pressure can be endured no more, until the words break loose from the mind attempting to retain them—precipitating the destruction of the old and hence making way for the creation of the new. But man insists on maintaining the link he has established with the past, and his "made-arch holds," "unshaken."[23] The word "unshaken" here contrasts ironically with the word "shaken" as used near the end of Section II (151:16–20).

The sequence that now occurs is centered upon three dogs, at least two of which have been consciously killed. The first was the pet of an individual identified as "Henry":

>Henry's the name. Just Henry,
>
>>ever'body
>knows me around here: hat
>pulled down hard on his skull, thick chested,
>fiftyish   .
>
>>I'll hold the baby.

23. The geography of the poem seems to be important here. Apparently Williams envisions that the bridge man builds between the present and the past (or perhaps even between the future and the past) acts as a sort of dam blocking the waters of the present moving beneath it.

The adjective "fiftyish" seems to suggest that Henry is the "Volunteer of America" who, earlier in the book (126:1–6), requests Paterson to give his prospective wife a blood test. If this is indeed so, the seemingly unimportant reference to the baby is a reaffirmation of the creative love which he represents, and his relationship to his dog may be understood as a manifestation of this love on another level. The infant's presence, too, combines with Henry's childlike manner of speaking to characterize him as a symbol of natural innocence:

> That was your little dog bit me last year.
> Yeah, and you had him killed on me. . . .
>
> You reported him and
> they come and took him. He never hurt
> anybody. . . .
>
> I bin nipped
> hundreds of times. He never done anybody any
> harm.

Something may of course be said for the man whom the dog has bitten (not necessarily Paterson himself). But that he uses the word "bit" instead of the word "nipped" seems, I think, to point up indifference and ultimate brutality on the part of the victimizer, rather than simply naïveté on the part of the victimized. That such indifference and brutality may in fact be disguised by conventionalized habits of language and action ("he *bit* me three times . . . I'm sorry but I *had/* to report him"—italics mine), only makes the situation worse.

The second dog in this sequence is not specifically identified and is characterized only as being "tense with the wine of death," moving "downstream/ on the swift current . . . turning/ upon the water." On the one hand, of course, this dog is related to Henry's dog, his fate being emblematic of destruction through the sheer momentum of conventional forms. On the other hand, however, the phrase "wine of death" imaginatively associates its death by water with something rich and strange.

This aspect of death is particularly important with respect to the sacrificial killing of Pogatticut's dog:

> Arrived at the burial place the funeral procession was met by Pogatticut's brothers and their followers. There was great lamentation and the Kinte Kay was performed in sadness.
>
> Wyandach, the most illustrious brother, performed the burial sacrifice. Having his favorite dog, a much loved animal, brought forth, he killed him, and laid him, after painting his muzzle red, beside his brother. For three days and three nights the tribes mourned   .

The chieftain himself—presumably "a man of gigantic stature" in the moral as well as in the physical sense—was clearly venerated and beloved by his tribe for the generous attitude he maintained toward them. And as with Henry, love of man is imaged in love for a dog. I assume that the ritual Wyandach performs has as a basic purpose Pogatticut's reunion with his dog after death. The contrast to the "necessary" killing of Henry's dog is therefore enormous: while in the former case societal forms lead to separation, in the latter they lead to a death-transcending union. To some extent, perhaps, this contrast is associated with a contrast between past and present, but Williams is ultimately concerned less with historical change than with opposing states of mind which are always present. This conclusion is supported by the relation of the Pogatticut passage to the previous prose passages concerning the Indians, and through them, to the Rasles chapter of *In the American Grain*.

The dog-killing sequence is followed by an episode concerning the killing of an invisible cat. The importance of this curious passage lies primarily in the fact that every viewpoint is ironically limited. On the simplest level there are the superstitions and witch hunts permeating the Van Giesen's society. Such attitudes, at least so the prose writer wishes us to believe, are the products of self-deluding minds:

> That Jane was bewitched was the belief of the whole neighborhood. Moreover, the witch who exercised this spell, and who made these weird visits to the sufferer, in the guise of a cat invisible to everybody but the bewitched, was believed to be Mrs. B. who lived in the gorge in the hill beyond. . . . Talking the matter over with his neighbors, Merselis (he was called "Sale") was told if he could shoot the spectral cat with a silver bullet he would kill the creature, and put a stop to the spells exercised over his wife.

As we have seen, Williams also presents situations such as this in *In the American Grain* (81–104). There, however, the accounts of "curiosities" and "wonders" are presumably from Cotton Mather's pen directly, the irony surrounding them coming only from the context in which Williams has embedded them. In *Paterson III* the "authorship" is more complicated, for here it is emphasized that a latter-day sophisticate (other than Williams) is preparing a history from previous sources: "About Merselis Van Giesen a *curious story illustrative* of the *superstition of the day* is to this effect" (italics mine). However, although the writer overtly stresses that the present *in* which he is writing is not the past *about* which he is writing, his position is not ultimately detached. Even though ostensibly ironic, his language nonetheless indicates a kind of half-belief in the very thing he is attacking. Particularly telling is the sentence with which the prose writer closes his account, for, while utterly irrelevant to what has come before, it characterizes his "sophistication" as merely the sophistication of the conventional pragmatist: "Merselis Van Giesen was assessed in 1807 for 62 acres of unimproved land, two horses and five cattle."

The third viewpoint represented in the sequence is that of the poet who inserts clever comments (in larger type) at appropriate points in the narrative. He is sufficiently aware to generalize the situation ("Are we any better off?") and to understand the irony of the prose writer's position: "62 acres of unimproved land, two horses/ and five cattle—/ (that cures the fantasy)." But his position is itself ironic in its inability to recognize the ambiguity of attacking the Van Giesens' vision at all:

> —what a picture of marital fidelity! dreaming
> as one.

The next three and a half pages are extremely difficult. As far as I know, the only critic who has attempted to justify them, indeed to comment on them at all, is Roy Harvey Pearce, who, in support of his belief that *"Paterson,* after Book I, in which the poet so clearly defines his own situation and its limits, appears to be disintegrative," tells us that this tendency finds its culmination on page 164, where "the lines are set crisscross on the page, literally imaging the imminent death drive of Dr. Paterson's world."[24] Although such an observation, as far as it goes, is true, we must also remember that in Williams' poetry destruction and disorganization are always associated with reconstruction. The "disintegration" page itself dwells on words and images associated not only with death (the blowing of a fuse, flowing, and funerals), but also, and often paradoxically with life, rebirth, and order (the "minute-glass . . . for timing eggs," the sign in the florist's window advertising "Funeral designs," "Wedding bouquets," and "Plants"—and "it should be explained," Williams adds, "that/ in this case 'plants' does NOT refer to interment"). *Paterson,* then, is considerably more than a simple mimesis of disintegrating culture and language.

Let us consider the content of these pages in somewhat greater detail. Clearly, they are a manifestation of a local event in the poem (the flood)[25]—as much as they are a manifestation of any more general tendency. As we have seen, one aspect of the flood is asso-

24. *American Poetry,* pp. 121, 124.
25. See 161:27–162:24.

ciated with the "leaden" weight symbolized by books and libraries.[26] The line with which the sequence opens, then,

The Book of Lead,

he cannot lift the pages

brings us back to the situation of 156:18–157:4. Weighted down by the stream grown leaden within him and anchored to his chair (note that "lift" is used here instead of "turn" as we might expect). Paterson has become a kind of book, thus experiencing the fate of the "white-hot" men who "decayed" into books. The flood is "still rising," and as the deadline for escape approaches, images of frustration occur more and more frequently:

He feels he ought to *do* more. He had
a young girl there. Her mother told her,
Go jump off the falls, who cares?—
She was only fifteen. He feels so frustrated.
I tell him, What do you expect, you
have only two hands   .   ?

But out of fear man suppresses the energy which is his only salvation:

It was a place to see, she said, The White Shutters. He said
I'd be perfectly safe there with him. But I never went. . . .
But one night they came leaping downstairs from the banquet

26. Cf. the following passage from Wallace Stevens' essay on "The Figure of the Youth as Virile Poet" (*The Necessary Angel,* p. 63):

He [the youth] says, so that we can all hear him: "I am the truth, since I am part of what is real, but neither more nor less than those around me. And I am imagination, in a leaden time and in a world that does not move for the weight of its own heaviness." . . . with his sense of the heaviness of the world, he feels his own power to lift, or help to lift, that heaviness away . . . to exercise his power to the full and at its height . . . to rely on his imagination.

hall tearing their clothes off, the women throwing their skirts over their heads, and joined in the dancing, naked, with the others on the main floor. He took one look and then went out the back window just ahead of the police, in his dress shoes into the mud along the river bank.

We are reminded of the "Beautiful Thing" episodes, particularly the first, Mary's spirited dance in Book II, and the early lyric called *Dance Russe* (*CEP* 148), in which the poet sings of dancing "naked, grotesquely/ before my mirror/ waving my shirt round my head/ and singing softly to myself." The phrase beginning this paragraph ("It was a place to see") is echoed twice in the lines which follow:

> Let me see, Puerto Plata is
> the port of Santo Domingo. . . .
>
> I see things,   .   .

"Seeing" is of course associated with "vision," but in these three passages the essential point is rather the opposition of "seeing" to "doing." Even questioning would be preferable to no activity at all, but like Tennyson's mechanical and ultimately indifferent cavalrymen, these men would rather "ask no whys," reasoning only that any possible objections to the status quo would be useless:

> There is no ease.
> We close our eyes,
> get what we use
> and pay. He owes
> who cannot, double.
> Use. Ask no whys?
> None wants our ayes.

There is no ease from our fears because they are solipsistically self-imposed, constantly perpetuated by our refusal to "see" more than

a world of usury and materialism. But man must rise from beneath
the leaden weight of such a world; he must lift himself from the
library in which he has been anchored and seek a rebirth into a
world redeemed from its oppressive flood:

> But somehow a man must lift himself
> again —
>   again is the magic word   .
>   turning the in out :
> Speed against the inundation

After an ironic reference to one such time in the past, "a time
when/ they didn't want any whites/ to own anything," and after the
disintegration page which I have already discussed, such a rebirth
is thus reenacted in the poem.

Indicating that it is indeed the beginning of an entirely new
movement, the process of reorganization centers upon another exchange between two opposing voices. The "voices" used here, however, differ from those used previously, for the first is a letter and
the second is a geological table. The letter, of course, is from Ezra
Pound in St. Elizabeth's Hospital. "Papa" Pound has prepared a
"readin list," presumably only a part of an even longer one, for
Williams' guidance:

> re read *all* the Gk tragedies in
> Loeb.—plus Frobenius, plus
> Gesell plus Brooks Adams
> ef you ain't read him all.—
> Then Golding 'Ovid' is in Everyman lib.

The Frobenius that Pound has in mind is Leo Frobenius, the
German who announced in 1910 that he had conclusive proof
of the existence of Atlantis, who was a proponent of extreme
theories of cultural diffusion, and who attributed a common origin
to the cultures of Oceania and West Africa. Gesell is Silvio Gesell,

the German economist known especially for his plan, published as *The Natural Economic Order,* "to secure an uninterrupted exchange of the products of labor, free from bureaucratic interference, usury, and exploitation."[27] Brooks Adams originated the theory of the westward movement of culture, as well as a theory that American democracy, particularly as a result of its great wealth, is by nature foreordained to degradation and decay. These are all writers, then, who would, in one way or another, interest both Pound the abstract "economist" and Pound the professed "world culture-bearer." When they are combined with the classical writers symbolized by the "definitive" translations of Ovid and the Greek tragedians, the representation of Pound's many-sided mind is virtually complete. But though Pound's "readin list" may suit his own aesthetic, it most certainly does not suit Williams'. Even Pound himself seems to know this, and the letter's humor is due only partly to the context in which Williams has placed it.

Man's true salvation is imaged in the second "voice," the report of an early well-digging:

SUBSTRATUM

Artesian well at the Passaic Rolling Mill, Paterson

The following is the tabular account of the specimens found in this well, with the depths at which they were taken, in feet. The boring began in September, 1879, and was continued until November, 1880.

This is, of course, yet another instance of descent—the "descent once more, to the ground . . . *the* ground, the only ground that he knows, that which *is* under his feet" (*Grain* 213). By "ground,"

27. *The Autobiography of William Carlos Williams* (New York, Random House, 1951), p. 385.

of course, Williams means more than simply "dirt," but as the tabulation shows, even that is rich in variety and interest:

DEPTH	DESCRIPTION OF MATERIALS
65 feet. . .	Red sandstone, fine
110 feet. . .	Red sandstone, coarse
182 feet. . .	Red sandstone, and a little shale
400 feet. . .	Red sandstone, shaly
404 feet. . .	Shale
430 feet. . .	Red sandstone, fine grained
540 feet. . .	Sandy shale, soft . . . etc.

We are reminded of the account of the lake-draining in Book I (46:28–47:37): "There were millions of fish," but "nobody dreamt of the quantity that were living in it." In an acquisitive society such as ours, however, men have eyes only for pragmatic ends:

> At this depth the attempt to bore through the red sandstone was abandoned, the water being altogether unfit for *ordinary use.* . . . The fact that the rock salt of England, and of some of the other salt mines of Europe, is *found* in rocks of the same age as this, raises the question whether it may not also be *found* here.   [italics mine]

As Williams puts it near the beginning of Section III (156:10–11), "The well that gave sweet water/ is sullied"—and sullied to a large extent by the "leaden flood" of a use-oriented, appropriative culture ("to the teeth, to the very eyes"). Nonetheless, to the imaginative man who would accept it, *Paterson* offers a faith in "the ground" as a source of ultimate hope. Pound's alternative is illusory. In spite of his pragmatic attempt at intellectual comprehensiveness (the word "all" is used three times in Pound's letter), the wealth of local particulars escapes him. Digging only into the past, he would establish an art based on the principle of spatial and temporal continuity. But Williams sees such an art as a perverting of the local, as an obscuring "by a field of unrelated culture" what he considers to be "the primitive destiny of the land." It is "imperative that we sink," for "where foreign values are held to be a desideratum, he who is buried and speaks thickly—is lost" (*Grain* 212).

From this point on, Section III exhibits an order in direct contrast to the disintegration imaged before. The completion of the process of reorganization is announced by the appearance of:

FULL STOP

—and leave the world
to darkness
and to
me.

The use of the fourth line of Gray's *Elegy* (except for the form of the verb) reminds us not only of the plowman's intimacy with the ground but also of his potential, if obscure, imaginative power. There is, then, an almost "witty" suggestion of a kind of confident Adamic[28] isolation amid a world of chaos.

This chaos, of course, remains as a direct consequence of the flood:

When the water has receded most things have lost their
form. They lean in the direction the current went. Mud
covers them
—fertile(?)mud.

Owing primarily to the ambiguity associated with the flood, these lines may be taken in two very different ways. On the one hand, they are another statement of Williams' belief that conventional

28. See R. W. B. Lewis, *The American Adam: Innocence, Tragedy, and Tradition in the Nineteenth Century* (Chicago, 1958), esp. pp. 1–53, 195–98.

forms pervert and obscure nature; as the Poundian-Eliotic aesthetic bends the present to make it continuous with a theoretical past, so cultural and societal restraints mold it to make it uniformly consistent. On the other hand, the flood is also associated, although to a lesser extent, with the "creative destruction" symbolized by fire. The covering of "fertile(?)mud" embodies these same ambiguities. In Section II (148:23–149:12) we have already read that the dead books are only "a nothing, surrounded by/ a [glistening] surface," an image which itself recalls the "field of unrelated culture stuccoed upon [the primitive destiny of the land]" associated with the aesthetic of Pound and Eliot. Again, however, we must also remember the contrary possibility suggested by the descriptions of the mauled bottle's "new glaze." The contrasting associations of mud with restrained hiding and with a generous and wholehearted giving of oneself to a "natural" vitality, are also implicit in the contrast between the "mud along the river bank," into which the owner of *The Clipper Crew* flees "just ahead of the police."

It is important to note, however, that with reference to our world, the two sides of this paradox are not equally weighted; the negative implications are ultimately the more applicable:

> If it were only fertile. Rather a sort of muck, a detritus,
> in this case—a pustular scum, a decay, a choking
> lifelessness—that leaves the soil clogged after it,
> that glues the sandy bottom and blackens stones—so that
> they have to be scoured three times when, because of
> an attractive brokenness, we take them up for garden uses.
> An acrid, a revolting stench comes out of them, almost one
> might say a granular stench—fouls the mind   .

Here we are back amid the images associated with the library: sterility, foulness, and oppressive stench. As we would expect, the "attractive" stones are appropriated for practical ends rather than contemplated aesthetically for what they are in themselves. And before they can even be "used," they must be polished so that "the surface/ glistens," so that their blackness—which paradoxically signifies both their corruption (a result of the muddy stream) and their inherent value (cf. 103:11–12 and 127:28–29)—is obscured.

Still, the poet-protagonist can and must transcend the inherent corruption of his world:[29]

> How to begin to find a shape—to begin to begin again,
> turning the inside out : to find one phrase that will
> lie married beside another for delight   .   ?
> —seems beyond attainment   .

To marry phrases together for delight involves much more than the mere art of surprising and paradoxical juxtaposition. Indeed, on the part of both poet and reader it requires the capacity for imaginative "wonder," which is in turn a mode of love. Rebirth, whether in life or poetry, is not easy,[30] but it can be approached through love, marriage, and delight: "However hopeless it may seem, we have no other choice: we must go back to the beginning; it must all be done over; everything that is must be destroyed" (*Grain* 215).

Resolution of the poem's tensions is still delayed, however, and we get only the ambiguous statement that *"American poetry is a very easy subject to discuss for the simple reason that it does not exist."* I am not certain whether we are to take this as a statement of the poet himself or as another statement of the opposing "voice." In either case, "poetry" can refer to either the conventionally "literary" or to the truly imaginative. Similarly, that "American" poetry "does not exist" can mean either that art is by definition traditional and "European" or that what Williams means by "American" and what the world conventionally means by "poetry" are simply not compatible. Williams' own belief, of course, is that "poetic" is synonymous with "local" and "imaginative," and as we

29. Cf. also 162:12–16.
30. Cf. use of the word "attain" in regard to the "Beautiful Thing"—e.g. 148:4, 12.

have seen, such an aesthetic is conceived as a part of a particular kind of tradition, an American tradition, the beginning of which Williams symbolizes in Poe:

> Poe's work strikes by its scrupulous originality, *not* "originality" in the bastard sense, but in its legitimate sense of solidity which goes back to the ground, a conviction that he *can* judge within himself. . . . It is the New World, or to leave that for the better term, it is a *new locality* that is in Poe assertive; it is America, the first great burst through to expression of a re-awakened genius of *place*. . . . On him is FOUNDED A LITERA-TURE—typical; an anger to sweep out the unoriginal, that became ill-tempered, a monomaniacal driving to destroy, to annihilate the copied, the slavish, the FALSE literature about him. . . . Poe could look at France, Spain, Greece, and NOT be impelled to copy. [*Grain* 216–33]

The statement in *Paterson* that American poetry does not exist may therefore mean that it does not exist now, but that a poet's new beginning in the present will be a "beginning *again*," combining in the process both past and present into a continuous present.

Unimaginative man, however, understands neither "poetry" nor "tradition," and sees American poetry only as corrupt,

> Degraded. The leaf torn from
> the calendar. All forgot.

As a solution he would "give/ it over to the woman," to "let *her*/ begin again" (italics mine). The "woman" here is clearly not the girl who figures earlier as the "Beautiful Thing." On the contrary, she is associated with energy gone stale, with the lifeless books that white-hot men become:

> Who is it spoke of April? Some
> insane engineer. There is no recurrence.

> The past is dead. Women are
> legalists, they want to rescue
> a framework of laws, a skeleton of
> practices, a calcined reticulum
> of the past which, bees, they will
> fill with honey   .

The first line here is almost certainly a reference primarily to *The Waste Land* (rather than to *The Canterbury Tales*), and Eliot and Pound are consequently associated with a kind of feminine passivity in contrast to a more masculine creativity. They write of confining cycles of continuity which are contrived, and they force the present to conform to a dead past instead of preserving the "presentness" of the past in a living present. The women, then, symbolize a very special kind of unimaginative men.[31] Out of fear they would rely on a framework of convention and restraint from the past, the interstitial spaces of which they would fill with the illusory honey of eclecticism.

At any rate, "The leaves—that were varnished/ with sediment" (cf. 167:8–11)—the leaves of the books of "legalists" and "poets" as well as the leaves torn from calendars—are now "fallen." "The flood has done its work," and what was already "clutter," "decay" has now made utterly "piecemeal." The unimaginative "voice" sees this as a disaster, of course, but the poet sees it as the prelude to rebirth. A "digestion" can now take place—not a digestion in the sense of "digest-making" associated with this word at 149:4 and 156:25, but a digestion in the sense of the "metamorphosis" which follows "dispersal." The women "want to rescue too much." But "It is not to be done." We must "build no more/ bridges" between the old world and the new, between past and present. The only hope lies in the local particulars of our existence ("of this, make it of *this,* this/ this, this, this, this") and in the energetic spontaneity with which these particulars must be aesthetically perceived,

31. Cf. the poetess and the "She" of Book II.

> ... Let the words
> fall any way at all—that they may
> hit love aslant. It will be a rare
> visitation.

As the section moves to its climax, the theme of an eternal present becomes more and more dominant. After the section just quoted, for example, there occurs a passage concerning a "fossil conch" whose primary[32] purpose is to deprecate the "baked melange" which is the "shelly rime" of Eliotic verse:

> Here's a fossil conch (a paper weight
> of sufficient quaintness) mud
> and shells baked by a near eternity
> into a melange, hard as stone, full of
> tiny shells
> —baked by endless desiccations into
> a shelly rime—turned up
> in an old pasture whose history—
> even whose partial history, is
> death itself.

Most of the images and themes involved here (weight, mud, stones, echoing of the past) I have already discussed, but I might note that there may be a pun on "shelly" as well as on "rime" ("melange" can connote harmony as well as hodgepodge), and that the "old pasture whose history . . . is death" may well be the Waste Land itself. The "sweet woman" must be abandoned ("either I abandon you or give up writing"), for as with the ambiguously delicate cherimoya, the fruit which Mark Twain called "deliciousness itself," sweetness is related to poison.

> ... After all, the slums
> unless they are (living)
> wiped out they cannot be re-
> constituted .

32. The contemplative/appropriative opposition is also involved of course.

> The words will have to be rebricked up, the
> —what? What am I coming to .
>   pouring down?

The question here is of course rhetorical. Yet before the final answer at the end of the book, there occurs one last prose section, describing the death rites of the African Ibidio:

> When an African Ibidio man is slain in battle, married women who are his next of kin rescue the corpse. . . . They lay him on a bed made of fresh leaves. Then they cut young branches from a sacred tree and wave the bough over the genital organs of the warrior to extract the spirit of fertility into the leaves. . . . Only married women, who have felt the fertility of men in their bodies, can know the secret of life.

It is important to note that the women taking part in the ceremony are "married women"; being the "wives of warriors," they thus symbolically embody the knowledge and attributes of both sexes and are not at all to be associated with the women discussed above. Somewhat paradoxically perhaps, these women represent the poet who is simultaneously a man married to a woman and a woman married to a man.[33] They embody beauty, energy, love, and the principle of fertility, and hence have the power to extract the life principle into the leaves. The "chant" which accompanies the ceremony is presumably

>   . . . a sort of praise, a
>   peace that comes of destruction[34]

which accompanies the burial of Pogatticut.

33. Cf. "A Note on *Paterson: Book III*," dated Sept. 28, 1949, which is printed on the dust jacket of the first edition of this book: *"Paterson* [sic] is a man (since I am a man) who dives from cliffs and the edges of waterfalls, to his death—finally. But for all that he is a woman (since I am not a woman) who *is* the cliff and the waterfall. She spreads protecting fingers about him as he plummets to his conclusions to keep the winds from blowing him out of his path. But he escapes, in the end, as I have said."

34. It is interesting to note that the "peace" here is not an Eliotic "Peace

Book III concludes with a formalized lyric of immensely moving power. It consists of eight four-line "stanzas" followed by a brief coda-like ending, the organization of which might be roughly schematized as ABA. The first stanza states that the poet's "sole" concern must be with an eternal present:

> The past above, the future below
> and the present pouring down: the roar,
> the roar of the present, a speech—
> is, of necessity, my sole concern   .

I have already discussed the symbolic meanings Williams attaches to the course of the Passaic River, to "the river above the Falls, the catastrophy [sic] of the Falls itself, the river below the Falls and the entrance at the end into the great sea."[35] The stanza presents few if any difficulties, but a sentence from the *Autobiography* is interesting in connection with it: "The Falls let out a roar as it crashed upon the rocks at its base. In the imagination this roar is a speech or a voice, a speech in particular; it is the poem itself that is the answer" (392). The roar of the Falls is a speech, having a meaning in itself, not simply a voice, the "meaning" of whose speech is inaccessible.[36] A poem like *Paterson,* then, as another roaring of the present (though "in wax"—i.e. in an artistic medium), is the "answer" to what the Falls is saying precisely because it is the Falls' echoing "replica," an imitation "made" out of the language and the events of the present.

Although ultimately generalized, the second stanza recalls several events from previous books:

> They plunged, they fell in a swoon
> or by intention, to make an end—the

---

which passeth understanding," but rather a peace that comes directly out of a creative destruction in the here and now.

35. "News from New Directions," May 31, 1951.

36. Cf. 135:9–12, 138:20–21.

> roar, unrelenting, witnessing .
> Neither the past nor the future.

Mrs. Cumming presumably "fell in a swoon," but as Williams makes clear in *Paterson* and elsewhere,[37] her death was highly ambiguous. Mr. Cumming would have "plunged into the abyss" behind her as a suicide. The "hoodlums and men" who "leaped into the mud" of the drained lake, even though admirably seeking the ground, were also seeking a pragmatic end in their plunge. Similarly, Sam Patch's goal was purely that of the diving itself. In contrast to all these, the poet seeks a symbolic plunge to make a new beginning, considering the descent to the ground not as an end in itself but as only a prelude to rebirth.

The poet's concern with the present is his "sole" concern, then, only in a very special sense. The Falls or the poem witnesses neither the past nor the future, not because these inaccessible temporal states are simply excluded, but because they are ultimately made one with the present (note that the subject of "is" in line 4 of the first stanza is ambiguous). This is especially true with respect to the past, and as we have seen, Williams' whole ideal is to bring the past back to life through the vital approach and marriage of his aesthetic. Lest we forget that absorption into the present without the awareness of this fuller significance may be fatal, the poet includes the important third stanza:

> Neither to stare, amnesic—forgetting.
> The language cascades into the
> invisible, beyond and above : the falls
> of which it is the visible part—.

The present is the poet's concern because only in the present can he truly "live" or "be"; the future is as inaccessible as the past is dead. But the visible present is nonetheless connected to the invisible

37. *Autobiography*, p. 394.

realms of both past and future, and it is indeed the time in which they can become visible themselves. The Falls, the language, poetry, and the mind, regardless of their immediacy, are therefore not wholly isolated from what is either "beyond" or "above."[38]

These important qualifications of the poet's original statement are continued in lines 20b–23a of the lyric. Of obviously greater importance, however, is the slightly different desire to be free from the conventions and restraints of the past. This is the primary theme of *Paterson* III, and it comes to its climax in the lines which make up the book's conclusion:

> . . . I cannot stay here
> to spend my life looking into the past:
>
> the future's no answer. I must
> find my meaning and lay it, white,
> beside the sliding water: myself—
> comb out the language—or succumb
>
> —whatever the complexion. Let
> me out! (Well, go!) this rhetoric
> is real!

"Here," of course, refers to the Infernal library in which Paterson has been voluntarily confined since the book's beginning. The "meaning" which he "must find," being "white" like the foamy spray itself, is ultimately identical with the "Beautiful Thing" in the white lace dress. Any traces of "guilt" he may "share" with the "sweet woman" of deception will be purified away through his association with the meaningless meaning of the "holy" girl ("Take off your clothes and purify/ yourself   .   ./ And let me purify myself/ —to look at you"—128:17–20). The rhetoric that is "real" is the language of marriage and love in the present.

38. It is important to remember in this regard that Williams conceives the Falls as moving both up and down at once, not just downward as it does in "reality."

4.

The Run to the Sea:

PATERSON,
BOOK
FOUR

The first section of *Paterson* IV, in both form and content, is a modern version of the "Theocritan" pastoral idyll.[1] The simplest kind of pastoral, of course, presents a nostalgic picture of an earlier, uncomplicated mode of life, drawn by a poet living in a later, more complex world. In such pastoral the oppositions between past and present, country and town, nature and art, the contemplative and the active are not ambiguous, but are treated quite simply, for it is assumed without question that an age once existed untainted by the deterioration and artificiality of the present. In Williams' pastoral, then, there is considerable emphasis on the deterioration, an emphasis that is pointed up by the very fact that the scene is New York City rather than Paterson. To be sure, "a perverted but still recognizable 'happy' picture of the past, is," at least by implication, "there," but it "is a sad picture today. It shows a desire to achieve all that we most hope for in the world. We all share the world together, we none of us possess it to ourselves. We WANT to share it. Only because we are thwarted do we fail to achieve our release."

1. See the letter written to Marianne Moore, June 23, 1951, in *Selected Letters,* p. 305. This letter is the source of all quotations in this paragraph.

As we might expect, however, Williams' attitude toward this deterioration is more closely akin to the relatively complex modes of pastoral. Unlike a Pound or an Eliot—"men that ran . . . off toward the peripheries to other centers, direct —/ for . . . loveliness and authority"—he approaches his world with an attitude of reconciliation, with the imaginative conviction that meaning and value must be found in the local present or not at all. To such an attitude William Empson's definition of complex pastoral is applicable, especially if we understand by the word "pretend" the connotations of simultaneous making and finding associated with the word "invent": "in pastoral you take a limited life and pretend it is the full and normal one, [suggesting] that one must do so with all life, because the normal is itself limited."[2] Hence Williams' generously sympathetic attitude toward "Corydon," the Lesbian poetess who epitomizes the sterile sophistication and artificiality represented by "the great city." "To me," the poet writes to Marianne Moore,[3] "the normal world is something which to you must seem foreign. I won't defend my world. I live in it." The Lesbian, in fact, seems less a free agent of choice than a pathetically helpless victim of chance. Thus, though she is clearly an agent of that which Williams abhors, as an individual she may be understood, pitied, even loved.[4] As Williams puts it in a letter to Robert Lowell,[5] "I like the old gal . . . she was at least cultured and not without feeling of a distinguished sort. I don't mind telling you that I started writing of her in a satiric mood—but she won me quite over. I ended by feeling admiration for her and real regret at her defeat." And in the letter of June 19 to Marianne Moore: "She has a hard part to play, and to my mind plays it rather well. . . . She is informed, no sluggard, uses her talents as she can."

2. *Some Versions of Pastoral* (Norfolk, Conn., New Directions, 1960), pp. 110–11.

3. June 19, 1951, in *Selected Letters*, p. 304. The symbolic association between the Lesbian and the city is also alluded to in this letter.

4. See "News from New Directions," May 31, 1951.

5. 1951, in *Selected Letters*, p. 302.

Phyllis, the young masseuse-nurse, is to Corydon, her employer, as the country wench of the traditional *pastourelle*[6] is to her courtly would-be seducer: the relationship is merely transposed into a rather startlingly modern key. Tellingly, Phyllis' "home" is not New York, or even Paterson, but Ramapo, a place where, as we are told some 150 pages earlier, "a bold association of wild and cultured life grew up together" (21:12–14). But although Phyllis is apparently attached to her alcoholic father with something more than ordinary daughterly love, and maintains, when queried by her employer, that she is "not . . . ashamed of her origins," she *has* left Ramapo for New York and refuses to return until her father promises "to cut out the booze." The young nurse, in other words, embodies a rather vulgar but natural energy, and her migration to the city seems emblematic of man's repudiation of the local. As her numerous letters to her father indicate, she is simultaneously repelled by sordidness of the "home" ("Maybe your family did once own the whole valley. Who owns it now?") and attracted by the prospects of materialistic and egotistical gain ("I'm having a fine time in the Big City as a Professional Woman, ahem! Believe me there's plenty of money here."). She does not, of course, understand either her actions or her motives, for they are essentially unconscious. Indeed, as her reference to the "fine time" she is having suggests, she is at this stage merely playing a game. But her flirtation with "the Big City" is dangerous, easily becoming the prelude to a repetition of her employer's fate. In a specific sense the forces leading her to destruction are the same forces that Williams sees leading American poetry to destruction, but in a more general sense they are also the forces leading to the defeat of imagination and love.

I turn now to a closer look at the text itself. Structurally, it is composed of twenty-one short subdivisions: nine dialogues between Phyllis and Corydon, five letters from Phyllis to her father, six

6. For an excellent, concise account of this form, including its important history, see the introduction to Frank Kermode's anthology of *English Pastoral Poetry: From the Beginnings to Marvell* (London, George G. Harrap, 1952), pp. 32–35.

scenes between Phyllis and Paterson, and one passage involving "the poet." Though these labeled divisions alternate in a more or less formal pattern, Williams manages the juxtapositions so as to obtain maximum dramatic effect. The section's form, in fact, comes very close to being that of a play. In the first scene, which is concerned with the beginning of the relationship between Phyllis and Corydon, the poet introduces a major theme of the whole book: "the perverse confusions that come of a failure to untangle the language and make it our own."[7] Corydon promises, for example, "Some day" when they "know each other better," to tell Phyllis "a few things," presumably the "long story" of her plight. As we might expect, however, she never really does, for the only language she knows is the "foreign" language of modern, "literary" verse. As Sister Bernetta has pointed out,[8] this failure of language is admirably summed up in Corydon's use of the adjective "silly" in the first line ("Two silly women!"). In Anglo-Saxon times "silly" meant "happy,"[9] and in later times the word came to be peculiarly associated with the happy simplicity of pastoral.[10] Here, however, the word has been "drained of its meaning"; it is not even adequate in its common modern meaning of "foolish." Corydon's use (or misuse) of the word, then, points up both the nature of her failings and the pathos of her plight. Indeed, the irony of the usage lies in the fact, unbeknownst to the poetess, that "silly" may also mean "helpless" or "pathetic."

In the next scene between Corydon and Phyllis (it is apparently the next day), Corydon attempts to make use of Phyllis' dissatisfac-

7. From the dust-jacket comment to the original edition of *Paterson* III.

8. Quinn, *Metamorphic Tradition*, p. 118.

9. Williams indicates his awareness of this when he refers, in the June 23 letter to Marianne Moore (*Selected Letters*, p. 305), to an idyl as a "happy" picture of the past. See also 182:14–183:4.

10. As in these lines from Nicholas Breton's *pastourelle* "Phillida and Coridon"—1591 (see Kermode, p. 168): "Thus with many a pretty oath,/ Yea and nay, and faith and troth,/ Such as silly shepherds use,/ When they will not Love abuse;/ Love, which had beene long deluded,/ Was with kisses sweet concluded."

tion with Ramapo to lead their relationship in the directions in
which Corydon obviously wants it to develop.[11] Barely concealing
her indifference, she easily leads the conversation from "that horrid
place . . . Ramapo" to "a city . . . Paterson," where Phyllis trained
and which Corydon remembers chiefly as the birthplace of another
girl with "Wonderful hands," to New York and the view from
her elegant East Side studio:

> ......Go
> look out of that window   .
>
> That is the East River. The sun rises there.
> And beyond, is Blackwell's Island. Welfare Island,
> City Island   .   whatever they call it now   .
> where the city's petty criminals, the poor
> the superannuated and the insane are housed   .

From here it is a relatively easy transition to more personal matters.
It is important to note, however, that Corydon needs Phyllis to fill an
aesthetic void as much as—perhaps even more than—she needs her
to fill a psychological void. Hence the important lines that follow:

> —and then
> the three rocks tapering off into the water   .
> all that's left of the elemental, the primitive
> in this environment. I call them my sheep   .

In "the great world" represented by the metropolis, the "elemental
character of the place" is, at least to the poetess, almost totally obscured. Where Williams finds and creates real meaning even in the
"modern replicas," she can only sentimentalize. The poet, like Phyllis,
would start from the thing itself—"They [the rocks] are white all

11. Cf. the courtier's traditional attitude toward the country girl, as well
as the pastoral poet's traditional right to utilize nature for his own artful
and/or artificial ends.

right but it's from the gulls that crap them up all day long"—though
unlike Phyllis, he would go on to loving and imaginative invention.
But to Corydon a direct confrontation of reality, a reality anything
but "docile," is impossible. In short, she yearns for Phyllis not only
out of her "lonesomeness" as a woman but also out of her "lonesomeness" as an artist. There is indeed great urgency in her plea:

> ... Be
> their shepherdess Phyllis. And I
> shall be Corydon   .   inoffensively, I hope?
> Phyllis and Corydon.   How lovely! Do you
> care for almonds?

The word "inoffensively" here is especially important, for although
it is somewhat ambiguous (inoffensive to whom?), the poetess does
seem sincere in using it. At one point, in fact, she specifically
refers to her relationship with Phyllis as a kind of innocent "play":
"Let's change names. You be Corydon! And I'll play Phyllis. Young!
Innocent! One can fairly hear the pelting of apples and the stomp
and clatter of Pan's hoofbeats. Tantamount to nothing" (187:8–11).
Ironically, of course, it would probably take far more even than
overt propositioning actually to offend Phyllis, and it is clear that her
understanding of her employer's psychological needs, let alone her
aesthetic needs, is minimal:[12]

> This is a racket, all I got to do is give her "massage"—and
> what do I know about massage? I just rub her, and how I rub
> her! And does she like it! And does she pay! Oh boy! . . .
>
> ... Do you
> care for almonds?

---

12. If complex pastoral idealizes nature, there is always in back of this
attitude a shadow of its opposite—the knowledge that nature may be rough
and that the natural life may be in fact rather an animal affair. This is, of
course, the old problem of the differences between a Ferdinand and a Caliban.

                    Nope, I hate all kinds of
       nuts. They get in your hair   .   your
       teeth, I mean   .

In the group of scenes that follows, the protagonist himself once
more enters the poem, as Phyllis' "lover." At the same time, however, Phyllis' inability to give herself wholly to him is hinted at by
her curious distinction between her "lover" and the "boy friend"
in whom she maintains she is "interested." As we learn later, it is
Paterson in whom she is really interested, but like the girl in the
second section of Book I (34:25–37:5), her desire is unacknowledged:

           . . . And what do you do together?

                    Just talk.

She does, of course, continually come to Paterson, and at one point
she even acknowledges "I like/ coming here, I need you" (199:20–
21). Indeed, her interviews with him recall, primarily through
verbal echoes, various scenes in Book III: the "maling and femaling"
of the "Beautiful Thing," the eventual revelation of her beauty (cf.
especially the repetition of the line, "Take off your clothes"—183:
20), and the mauling of the old bottle by the fire (cf. 188:4–6, 199:
11–13). But in the end, because of her solipsistic restraint, her visits
degenerate into a mere tease (e.g. 187:12–189:3), and even she "loses
out" (199:23–200:1). This is especially true in a symbolic sense, for
Phyllis ultimately represents " 'Paterson' in his young female phase,"
and, in her "impact . . . with a world beyond his own, limited in the
primitive, provincial environment," the "Paterson" who is her lover
would have been able to save her.[13] Significantly, she covers up her
fear of Paterson with another tangled perversion of language: "He's
married. I/ haven't got a chance with him."[14]

13. See the June 23 letter to Marianne Moore, in *Selected Letters*, p. 305.
14. Almost immediately, however, in a passage of rigorous self-mockery
(183:5–15), "the poet" undercuts even the positive implications of her
statement.

Except for the conclusion, the remainder of Section I is almost
entirely concerned with Corydon's recitation to Phyllis of some of
her "poetry"—first, two very brief prefatory lyrics, and then extended
excerpts from a long poem she calls *Corydon, a Pastoral*. If this poem
is a pastoral, however, it is a pastoral only of the most mundane
escapist sort, resting on the assumption that the world of the present
is unredeemably corrupt and must be repudiated in favor of a retreat
to a never-never-land of passivity and fantasy. The style of her poetry
therefore begins in a degenerate imitation of Eliot, mixed with tor-
tured hints of Crane:

<blockquote>

                        Condemned   .

But who has been condemned   .   where the tunnel
under the river starts? *Voi ch'entrate*
revisited! Under ground, under rock, under river
under gulls   .   under the insane   .

    .   the traffic is engulfed and disappears   .
to emerge   .   never

A voice calling in the hubbub (Why else
are there newspapers, by the cart-load?) blaring
the news no wit shall evade, no rhyme
cover. Necessity gripping the words   .   scouting
evasion, that love is begrimed, befouled . . .

                . . . the flesh a
flesh of tears and fighting gulls   .

            Oh I could cry!
cry upon your young shoulder for what I know.
I feel so alone   .

</blockquote>

and ends in a modulation toward early Yeats:

Come with me to Anticosti, where the salmon
lie spawning in the sun in the shallow water . . .
—and we shall fish for the salmon fish . . .
                    —and its silver
shall be our crest and guerdon.

To be sure, as Williams himself seems ironically to imply, such
poetry has its moments. Some of the imagery in the first passage
quoted above is, I think, extraordinary, and the echoes from the
Inferno and the Bible (especially in the image of the voice crying in
the wilderness of the modern hubbub) are very effective. But to
Williams such poetry is ultimately the poetry of death, particularly
suicide (note the recurrent references to the student suicide, "some
girl about [Phyllis'] age"—cf. 191:21–25, 189:1–6). As the style
of such poetry leads to the death of invention, so its content leads
to the death of imagination, love, and finally life. Significantly, Williams associates Corydon's milieu with the stagnation of the Library:
her studio "is full of books in all languages," and her poem "Stinks."

Corydon's poem, of course, functions solely to reveal its poet to
the reader of *Paterson;* it has no effect whatsoever on Phyllis. In a
way this is encouraging, for combined with the implications of her
last letter to her father [the guide "speaks french and the Missis talks
to him in that language. I don't know what they're saying (and I don't
care, I can talk my own language)"], and with the ambiguity of the
section's two concluding scenes, her "seduction" by sophistication
and artifice remains almost as inconclusive as her "salvation" through
her father and Paterson.

In Section II Williams turns from the themes of sterility and divorce to the more optimistic themes of fertility and marriage. Once
more weaving a lyrical meditation out of diverse memories and
imaginings, the poet disposes these elements into three distinct
groups: an introductory section centering upon a lecture on atomic
fission, a section centering upon the Curies' discovery of radium,
and a concluding section centering upon the word "credit."

In the first sequence Williams remembers attending the lecture with his son:

> You were not more than 12, my son
>   14 perhaps, the high school age
> when we went, together
>   a first for both of us,
> to a lecture, in the Solarium
>   topping the hospital, on atomic
> fission. I hoped to discover
>   an "interest" on your part.
> You listened   .

The "Solarium" (though of course a common name) here seems to be a kind of temple of the sun[15]—a shrine of Apollo, who is in many ways the presiding deity of the section. One of the section's major themes, in fact, and its richest source of metaphor is the ultimate equivalence of atomic physics (scientific devotion to the energy processes of the sun), medicine (the art of healing, easily extended to psychological and social, as well as physiological, ills), and poetry. The Solarium thus becomes not only the room atop the hospital but also Madame Curie's medical school laboratory and Dr. William Carlos Williams' own office.[16] It is telling that some of the section's most important imagery first occurs in *Paterson* III,[17] the book that deals "extensively with 'the flame'":[18]

>   As we approached the hospital
> the air above it, having taken up
>   the glow through the glass roof
> seemed ablaze, rivalling night's queen.

15. In overt contrast to a library or a university lecture hall.
16. An analogous ambiguity applies to the line, "The room was packed with doctors" (202:8).
17. Cf. 140:8, 131:24–133:9.
18. Letter to Babette Deutsch, July 28, 1947, in *Selected Letters*, p. 259.

Even more important than the Solarium is the action associated with it, "fission." The primary level of refence here is of course to the class of nuclear reactions in which a nucleus is split into smaller parts, with a simultaneous release of large amounts of energy. As applied to Williams' poetic theory and practice, this process is an ideal image for metamorphosing "dispersal," and it therefore takes on all the connotations of the Falls. Besides the dispersal of experience (cf. 201:10–17), some of the most important phases of this process are "the splitting of the poetic foot"[19] and the dispersal of traditional poetic forms (e.g. epic). All these processes, like nuclear fission itself, are processes of creative destruction, processes in which the fathering of division paradoxically results in creative metamorphosis. Such implications are also involved in another meaning of "fission"—namely, the sequence of cellular division, ultimately leading to birth, which is initiated by the union of sperm and ovum (a process itself analogous to the capture of an extranuclear particle by a nucleus prior to atomic fission).[20] Sexual images, particularly suggestions of the beginning of life, are consequently numerous.

Williams develops his theme through a reference to Billy Sunday, the evangelist who attempted to split "the atom of bitterness" by separating men from the "Puritan" aspects of the world and of himself (cf. the Evangelist of Book II), until he becomes "a split personality" (i.e. a "married" man halfway become "divorced"), and is "exhausted/ in his efforts to split . . . the [collection] plate" between two masters. Tellingly, he is associated with both Judas Iscariot and Alexander Hamilton. Then comes a letter from "A[lan] G[insberg],"[21] in which the "unknown young poet," who like

19. As Williams indicated in an early typescript of *Paterson*. See Thirlwall, "William Carlos Williams' *Paterson*," p. 273.

20. As pediatrician and father, Williams was profoundly impressed by the wonder and beauty of the beginning of life. The cover of the important volume *Kora in Hell: Improvisations* is in fact an extraordinary representation of just this process (see *I Wanted To Write a Poem*, pp. 28–29).

21. In the original (1951) edition of *Paterson* IV the letter is initialed "A.P."

Williams himself is seeking a metamorphosing dispersal of life and art, makes his presence known to the "unknown old poet" who is his literary father.

At this point the poet begins the superb sequence on the Curies' discovery of radium. Although this section is complex, it is not really obscure, but understanding it does require an awareness of a few basic aspects of natural radioactivity and of the historical circumstances surrounding the Curies' discovery. Specifically, "radioactivity" is the disintegration of the nucleus of an atom with the emission of energetic particles and rays. In atoms of uranium-238 this process occurs naturally at a precise, unchangeable rate, resulting in a continuous transmutation of random uranium atoms into atoms of another element. Some atoms of this element will then disintegrate into atoms of another element, some of these into atoms of yet another element, and so on, transmutation stopping only when atoms have become a stable (nonradioactive) form of lead. The rates of these different reactions vary widely: atoms of some of the elements in the series tend to disappear almost as soon as they are formed; atoms of other elements tend to last for longer periods, up to hundreds of thousands of years. In consequence, any pure sample of uranium-238 (containing uncountable billions of individual atoms) will, after very long periods of time (e.g. the age of the earth), become "contaminated" by various amounts of all the other elements in the series—by larger amounts of the elements whose atoms disintegrate at lower rates, by smaller amounts of the elements whose atoms disappear at higher rates. Radium, the most important element in the series, accumulates in relatively small concentrations, but since it is about a million times as radioactive as uranium itself, once-pure samples of uranium-238 will today, because of the formation even of extremely small quantities of radium, be considerably more radioactive than they were originally. In particular, pitchblende, the naturally occurring ore of such "contaminated" uranium, is approximately four times as radioactive as the amount of uranium seems to warrant. It was this discrepancy, in fact, that prompted Pierre and Marie Curie to subject several tons of pitchblende to a process involving more than ten thousand separate crystallizations and recrystallizations, in order ultimately to extract, in the form of radium chloride, the tiny percentage of radium (barely a few millionths of an ounce). The ordinary compounds of radium are all colorless, but they become colored ("stained") upon standing as a result of bombardment by radioactive particles, and are luminous in the dark.

Williams himself presumably learned these things from the lecture in the Solarium and from a motion picture on Madame Curie's life (202:20), and his poetry draws upon both sources. In the previous chapter I discussed the implications of the discovery only in terms of its difficulty; here I wish to develop its implications in terms of the more general themes of the whole section. Particularly important, especially in light of the "fission" symbol, are the continual suggestions that Madame Curie is with child:

> —a furnace, a cavity aching
> toward fission; a hollow,
> a woman waiting to be filled . . .

> . . . Curie, the man, gave up
> his work to buttress her.

> But she is pregnant! . . .

> —with ponderous belly, full
> of thought!

To be sure, the lines refer primarily to mental and imaginative fecundity, but these depend upon the various forms of love. The result of imagination and love, on many levels, is of course the invention of "wonder" and "beauty":

> Glory to God in the highest
> and on earth, peace, goodwill to
> men!

> Believe it or not.

As the section's basic imagery makes clear, however, creative love is paradoxically associated with "destructive" dispersal. In one sense, perhaps, this involves what Levy (Carlo Levi?) calls "antagonistic cooperation" (208:4–5), but the word "dissonance" is more accurate. As Williams uses the word, dissonance, like fission, involves an instability that is ultimately transcended by the discovery of new order in the metamorphic re-collection of dispersed particles:

> A dissonance
> in the valence of Uranium
> led to the discovery
>
> Dissonance
> (if you are interested)
> leads to discovery.

Significantly, this passage immediately follows the one quoted above, in which Madame Curie's "pregnancy" is associated with the miracle of Christ's birth (and of the universal love it might initiate) and with the "wonders" of Ripley's "Believe It or Not."

The metamorphosis that results from dissonance will probably assign value in new ways, or, as Williams puts it, it will

> . . . dissect away
> the block and leave
> a separate metal:
>
> hydrogen
> the flame, helium the
> pregnant ash   .

This is mainly a reference to the Curies' extraction of radium (quite literally, "a separate metal"), first from the pitchblende, and finally from the residue that remains in the distilling retort:

> ... the
> valence of Uranium inexplicably
> increased. ...
>
> But there may issue, a contaminant,
> some other metal radioactive
> a dissonance, unless the table lie,
> may cure the cancer   .   must
> lie in that ash   .   Helium plus, plus
> what? ...
>
>   and will at best take out
> its spate in mathematics
>   replacing murder.

"Helium" here refers to the alpha rays (helium nuclei) given off by the radium. It only *seems* to be all that the stain contains, however, for as Madame Curie discovered, "returning in the/ night," a minuscule amount of radium ("without weight") is there as well.[22] In another sense these lines present an emblem of the process of artistic abstraction, practiced by the poet as well as by the sculptor. This is, of course, the artist's means of releasing "the radiant gist."

The "wonderful" discoveries to which dissonance leads—as witnessed by Madame Curie's discovery of radium, by the poet's discovery of new meanings through the utilization of new forms and techniques (e.g. the "antagonistic cooperation" of poetry and prose—208:6–21), by a sensitive man's discovery of a new perspective on life after attending a disturbing lecture on modern science,[23] and even by Dr. Williams' discovery of "Salmonella montevideo" in a nurse who has "had no history of previous intestinal disturbance" —will ultimately "heal" man of his various physiological, social, and imaginative maladies, "the cancers" of "Puritanism" in our time.

22. The hydrogen may refer to the flame under the retort. The "flame," of course, is of great significance in its own right.
23. See Thirlwall, p. 273.

The poet believes this even though he recognizes that the way of success may be difficult and slow:

A man like you should have everything he wants   .

                not half asleep
        waiting for the sun to part the labia
        of shabby clouds   .   but a man (or
        a woman) achieved

                        flagrant!
        adept at thought, playing the words
        following a table which is the synthesis
        of thought, a symbol that is to him,
        sun up! a Mendelief, the elements laid
        out by molecular weight, identity
        predicted before found!

The first line here repeats the words of Phyllis, Paterson's inhibited mistress. In a letter to Parker Tyler,[24] Williams writes with respect to his difficulties in finding a "new way of measuring":

> I always think of Mendelejeff's table of atomic weights in this connection. Years before an element was discovered, the element helium, for instance, its presence had been predicated by a blank in the table of atomic weights.
>
> It may be that I am no genius in the use of the new measure I find inevitable; it may be that as a poet I have not had the genius to do the things I set up as essential if our verse is to blossom. I know, however, the innovation I predict must come to be. Someone, some infant now, will have to find the way we miss. Meanwhile I shall go on talking.

Ultimately, however, the lines quoted above apply to every discovery Williams is trying to make in or through his poem.

24. Feb. 9, 1946, in *Selected Letters*, pp. 242–43.

In the final part of Section II the poet further develops man's quest for meaning by again emphasizing the relationship of this quest to efforts to substitute generous, trusting love ("credit") for selfish, fearful exploitation ("usury"). Developing leads introduced in the second section of Book II (especially 90:19–27 and 92:22–93:9), Williams associates "usury" with the "money" which the Federal Reserve Banks "create from nothing."[25] Such "money" is a "JOKE," for it "could be wiped out/ at stroke/ of pen/ and was when/ gold and pound were/ devalued." Yet ultimately the "usury system" is worse than even the most vicious joke: it is a "crime," a "cancer" undermining true "value" at an ever "accelerated pace." For "Money sequestered enriches avarice, makes/ poverty: the direct cause of/ disaster." "Credit," however, which "makes solid" and "is related directly to the effort,/ work: value created and received," would remedy "the fallacies and illusions upon which [the usury system] is based." "Credit" is "the Parthenon"—that is, a work of loving and imaginative art—while "money" is merely "the gold entrusted to Phideas for the/ statue of Pallas Athena, that he 'put aside'/ for private purposes"—that is, a materialistic possession which is, at most, a physical medium out of which the work of art can be made. "Money" can be appropriated, but "You can't steal credit : the Parthenon." The giving of "credit"—to our fellow-man and to our world—is thus yet another metaphor for "invention," the "approach" Williams affirms throughout his poem. It is "THE GIST . . . 'the radiant gist' against all that/ scants our lives," which the "married" man must liberate from confining restraint through "fission" and "dispersal":

> Money: Uranium (bound to be lead)
> throws out the fire   .
> —the radium's the credit—the wind in
> the trees, the hurricane in the

25. Here, as in Book II, Williams echoes Pound in both style and content.

> palm trees, the tornado that lifts
> oceans   .
> Trade winds that broached a continent
> drive the ship forward . . .
>
> Let out the fire, let the wind go!
> Release the Gamma rays that cure the cancer
> .   the cancer, usury. Let credit
> out   .   out from between the bars
> before the bank windows.

The concluding section of Book IV is a final, powerful summary of Williams' myth. It opens, however, with a note of doubt, even despair, as the poet, now an old man, thinks back on all that has come before and wonders what, if anything, he has accomplished:

> Haven't you forgot your virgin purpose,
> the language?
>
> What language? "The past is for those who
> lived in the past," is all she told me.

Yet the tone here is very close to the tone of the letter of June 19 to Marianne Moore:

> If the vaunted purpose of my poem seems to fall apart at the end—it's rather frequent that one has to admit an essential failure. At times there is no other way to assert the truth than by stating our failure to achieve it. If I did not achieve a language I at least stated what I would not say. . . .
> But, if I did not succeed on one level, I did cling to a living language on another. The poem, as opposed to what was accomplished in the story, came to life at moments—even when my failure was most vocal and went above that to a different sort of achievement. Or so I believe.

Williams' assertions here are qualified, of course, but his qualifications are continually qualified themselves (particularly through the many *if's*), and it is clear that the poet believes he has, at least to some extent, "asserted the truth" not only in negative but also in positive terms. That the "past is for those who/ lived in the past" is "all" he has learned is thus likewise ambiguous, especially in light of the lyric that concludes *Paterson* III. The poet has also learned of the meaning and value available in the local present.

In addition, then, to that which the poet states he "would not say" (i.e. affirm), Section III also points up what he clearly would affirm. But before considering the more positive side of his statement, let us consider what he rejects—the meaning, that is, of the "sea" whose attractions he resists. On one level, of course, the sea is a symbol of the confining past, of the restraining conventions in life or literature that men follow, unquestioningly, merely because they *are* from the past. On another level, however, the sea is a symbol of a past whose influence is more ambiguous. Throughout the section the poet (Williams, Paterson the man) is reminded of episodes from his earlier life, episodes which seem to suggest that it is only in the past that love and harmony, beauty and vitality, are to be found. He remembers, for example, an incident of spontaneous, generous "approach":

—while [an old friend, now gone] was still in the hotel business, a tall and rather beautiful young woman came to his desk one day to ask if there were any interesting books to be had on the premises. He, being interested in literature, as she knew, replied that his own apartment was full of them and that, though he couldn't leave at the moment—Here's my key, go up and help yourself.

She thanked him and went off. He forgot all about her.

After lunch he too went to his rooms not remembering until he was at the door that he had no key. But the door was unlatched and as he entered, a girl was lying

naked on the bed. It startled him a little. So much so that all
he could do was to remove his own clothes and lie beside her.
Quite comfortable, he soon fell into a heavy sleep. She also
must have slept.

They wakened later, simultaneously,
much refreshed.

And there are reminiscences of the various girls he has loved:
"Margaret of the big breasts and daring eyes," "Lucille . . . who to
the amazement of many, married a saloon keeper and lost her
modesty," "loving Alma, who wrote a steady hand, whose mouth
never wished for relief," "the cold Nancy, with small firm breasts . . .
who never smiled more than was sufficient but whose broad mouth
was icy with pleasure," and, perhaps most important of all, the girl
who made him "believe in [Heaven]   .   a little." Yet all
these reminiscences are in the end only "souvenirs of childhood,"
and as Williams makes clear in the contrast between the two kinds
of pastoral in Section I, sentimental yearning after a lost golden
age, especially when combined with a refusal to seek value in the
present, is futile as well as reprehensible. The same also applies to
the reminiscence of the pastoral past of Paterson the city:

> In a deep-set valley between hills, almost hid
> by dense foliage lay the little village.
> Dominated by the Falls the surrounding country
> was a beautiful wilderness where mountain pink
> and wood violet throve: a place inhabited only
> by straggling trappers and wandering Indians. . . .
>
> The wigwam and the tomahawk, the Totowa tribe
> On either side lay the river-farms resting in
> the quiet of those colonial days: a hearty old
> Dutch stock, with a toughness to stick and
> hold fast, although not fast in making improvements.

Here again, the inherent attractiveness of the past may ultimately be dangerous, blinding man to the potentialities of reality.

In another sense the sea represents not so much a golden age of childhood and pastoral as a golden age of magnificent civilization. On the literary level this leads to a kind of Poundian exultation in the "splendor of renaissance cities" (i.e. eclectic and highly developed "Kulchur"), which reduces the present to the "squalor of spreading slums." The vocalization of this attraction is the cry of longing we have already heard in the agonized poem of Corydon:

> Oh that the rocks of the Areopagus had
> kept their sounds, the voices of the law!
> Or that the great theatre of Dionysius
> could be aroused by some modern magic
> > to release
> what is bound in it, stones!
> that music might be wakened from them to
> melt our ears . . .

> Thalassa! Thalassa!
> > Drink of it, be drunk!
> > Thalassa
> immaculata: our home, our nostalgic
> mother in whom the dead, enwombed again
> cry out to us to return   .
> > the blood dark sea!
> nicked by the light alone, diamonded
> by the light   .   from which the sun
> alone lifts undamped his wings
> > of fire!

In yet another sense the sea is the "sea of indifferent men."[26] On the one hand, Williams is here referring to what he calls, after

26. Thirlwall, p. 304.

Hamilton, "the great beast," the unimaginative and insensitive masses:

>   . . . There were
> others — half hearted, the over-eager,
> the dūll, pity for all of them, staring
> out of dirty windows, hopeless, indifferent,
> come too late and a few, too drunk
> with it — or anything — to be awake to
> receive it. All these
> and more — shining, struggling flies
> caught in the meshes of Her hair, of whom
> there can be no complaint, fast in
> the invisible net — from the back country,
> half awakened — all desiring. Not one
> to escape, not one   .   a fragrance
> of mown hay, facing the rapacious,
> the "great"   .

Ultimately, however, the sea of indifferent men also refers to "the great world" or "the great city." This is the world which presents to the local a façade of blasé sophistication, but which is, in reality, desperately trying to hide its fear and shame—the world, in short, of the Lesbian poetess. In either case, of course, the indifference is "the indifference of certain death."

All these meanings of the sea involve the "divorce" that to Williams is *the* characteristic of "Puritanism." As we have seen, the causes behind this divorce may vary, but in each case denial of spiritual value in approach to local particulars leaves the way open for material exploitation and appropriation. This applies to other men as well as to the rest of the local world, and exploitation may therefore take the forms of lust, murder, and war. On one final level, then, the sea represents the "sea of blood," witnessed not only by examples from the past—such as the savage massacre, in 1752, of the man called Jonathan (219:16–219:25), Fred Goodell's

murder of his six-month-old daughter, Nancy (220:9–26), and
John Johnson's "inhuman butchery," in 1850, of the aged Van
Winkle couple—but also by instances in the present, specifically
wars, like the Korean War, which broke out at the time Williams
was writing *Paterson* IV. He was, in fact, greatly disturbed by the
sudden, seemingly irrational outbreak of fighting, as a letter to
José García Villa[27] indicates:

> A cold east wind, today, that seems to blow from the other
> side of the world seems at the same time to be blowing all
> poetry out of life. A man wonders why he bothers to continue
> to write. And yet it is precisely then that to write is most im-
> perative for us. That, if I can do it, will be the end of *Paterson,*
> Book IV. The ocean of savage lusts in which the wounded shark
> gnashes at his own tail is not our home.
>
> It is the seed that floats to shore, one word, one tiny, even
> microscopic word, is that which can alone save us.

The Korean War, then, is the literal meaning of the impassioned
cry that follows:

> Murder.
>
>   —you cannot believe
> that it can begin again, again, here
> again   .   here
> Waken from a dream, this dream of
> the whole poem   .   sea-bound,
>   rises, a sea of blood . . .
>
> Turn back I warn you
>   (October 10, 1950)
> from the shark, that snaps
> at his own trailing guts, makes a sunset
> of the green water   .

27. 1950, in *Selected Letters,* pp. 291–92.

Yet in larger terms these lines refer to all wars and to the murder and death ultimately resulting from the absence of love and imagination in general.[28] What is perhaps most telling of all is that Williams regards even those wars that are "justified," in having as their avowed purpose the "ending" of war, as being as tragically ineffective and pitiful as the execution of a convicted criminal:

> John Johnson, from Liverpool, England, was convicted after 20 minutes conference by the jury. On April 30th, 1850, he was hung in full view of thousands who had gathered on Garrett Mountain and adjacent house tops to witness the spectacle.

You come today to see killed
                    killed, killed
    as if it were a conclusion
                    —a conclusion!
    a convincing strewing of corpses
    —to move the mind

                as tho' the mind
    can be moved, the mind, I said
    by an array of hacked corpses:

                        War!
    a poverty of resource   .   .

                Twenty feet of
    guts on the black sands of Iwo

28. It is significant that Jonathan was murdered by the "bayonettes" of "Tories" whom "some neighbor had led . . . to the attack, less from political or pecuniary considerations than from motives of private revenge." After "the murderers were gone, his wife and a neighbor took blood out of the bed in double handfuls." Totally incapable of even the most fundamental kind of parental love, Goodell "told the police he had killed [his daughter] by twice snapping the wooden tray of a high chair into the baby's face Monday morning when her crying annoyed him as he was feeding her."

> "What have I done?"
>
> —to convince whom? the sea worm?
> They are used to death and
> jubilate at it   .   .

The line "What have I done?," Johnson's only reaction when confronted with the scene of his atrocities, is almost certainly a moving allusion, on the part of the poet, to the forgiving pity of Christ: "Father, forgive them, for they know not what they do."

As the poem draws toward its conclusion, Williams' meditation becomes, as at other points of crisis in the poem, a dialogue between two interior voices. One voice, maintaining that "the run to the sea" is inevitable, that "The sea *is* our home whither all rivers/ (wither) run," would lead the poet to succumb to its attractions in apathetic despair:

> The ocean yawns!
> It is almost the hour . . .
>
> the nostalgic sea
> sopped with our cries
> Thalassa! Thalassa! . . .
>
> Yet you will come to it, come to it! The
> song is in your ears, to Oceanus
> where the day drowns . . .
>
> You will come to it, the blood dark sea
> of praise. You must come to it. Seed
> of Venus, you will return   .   to
> a girl standing upon a tilted shell, rose
> pink   .

But if man's struggle to resist the sea is difficult, he does resist it in the end:

I warn you, the sea is *not* our home.
    the sea is not our home . . .

I say to you, Put wax rather in your
ears against the hungry sea
    it is not our home.

Where, then, is our home? Clearly, it is on the continent, on the
ground, beside the sliding waters of the Falls. It is where the local
present is approached, not with indifference and appropriation, but
with imagination and love, where meaning is invented out of the
dispersal and metamorphosis of particulars. In such a home man is
free of the tyranny of a lost or outmoded past, and hence free to
make a new beginning as and where he lives.

To be sure, he may—indeed must—remain aware of his past; for
a full knowledge of his origins is vital to his freedom of choice. But
he will be as free from sentimentality as he is free from conventionality, and though he will seek to recover his (human and
humane) source, he will seek to do so only by bringing the past over
into the present. For example, with respect to "the early days of
Paterson," which Williams so vividly invokes in the latter parts of
Book IV, although "Many of the old names and some of the/ places
are not remembered now," they can be rediscovered in the present
by the loving and imaginative poet—in all of us. Thus, surrounded
by references to such places as "The Godwin/ Tavern, the most
historic house in Paterson,/ on River Street," and "a nail factory
where/ they made nails by hand . . . in what is now called the Old
Gun Mill Yard," and to the ruggedness and vitality of the "straggling
trappers and wandering Indians" who first inhabited the "beautiful
wilderness" of the surrounding country—in the very midst of these
passages Williams places the second letter from Alan Ginsberg:

Dear Doc: Since I last wrote I have settled down more, am
working on a Labor newspaper (N.J. Labor Herald, AFL) in

Newark. The owner is an Assemblyman and so I have a chance
to see many of the peripheral intimacies of political life which
in this neighborhood has always had for me the appeal of the
rest of the landscape, and a little more, since it is the landscape
alive and busy.

Do you know that the west side of City Hall, the street, is
nicknamed the Bourse, because of the continual political and
banking haggle and hassel that goes on there?

Also I have been walking the streets and discovering the
bars—especially around the great Mill and River streets. Do
you know this part of Paterson? I have seen so many things—
negroes, gypsies, an incoherent bartender in a taproom over-
hanging the river, filled with gas, ready to explode, the window
facing the river painted over so that the people can't see it. I
wonder if you have seen River Street most of all, because that is
really at the heart of what is to be known.

I keep wanting to write you a long letter about deep things
I can show you, and will some day—the look of streets and
people, events that have happened here and there.

The best gloss on this letter is perhaps the following sentence from
Ginsberg's first letter: "This place is as I say my natural habitat by
memory, and I am not following in your traces to be poetic: though
I know you will be pleased to realize that at least one actual citizen
of your community has inherited your experience in his struggle to
love and know his own world-city, through your work, which is an
accomplishment you almost cannot have hoped to achieve" (205: 13–
19). When discussing the meanings of the sea, I pointed out Williams' despair in the face of the seemingly eternal recurrence of
murder and divorce. The passage I was discussing, however, may
also apply to the recurrence of creation and marriage:

> —you cannot believe
> that it can begin again, again, here
> again   .   here.

To some extent, then, the meaning of the lines with which *Paterson* IV ends has to do with the principle of continuity through recurrence: though one form of the eternal poet has grown old, he has already metamorphosed into another. This is of course a version of one of the central Romantic myths: the rebirth of Apollo as an incarnation of the rebirth of poetry. Thus the image of the "seeds float[ing] in with the scum/ and wrack   .   among brown fronds/ and limp starfish"—seeds which, in contrast with the sterile, tightly closed seeds that Williams uses in *In the American Grain* to represent the sources of divorce, are the fertile seeds that will overcome the "wrack" and "words" of the great sea that would snare them, and blossom into the fullness of marriage.[29]

Yet in a very real sense, I think, this image of seeds, the book's closing lines, and even Alan Ginsberg's letter may be applied to Williams himself, for all involve the "eternal" life of the loving imagination. Like the Falls, which continuously falls and refalls, he is continually reborn in the infinitely expanded interval of his life. Thus, although the attraction of the sea would impel him, like the Whitman of *Out of the Cradle, Endlessly Rocking,* to embrace as final reality the time-bound principles of necessity and death:

> My serpent, my river! genius of the fields,
> Kra, my adored one, unspoiled by the mind,
> observer of pigeons, rememberer of
> cataracts, voluptuary of gulls! Knower
> of tides, counter of hours, wanings and
> waxings, enumerator of snowflakes, starer
> through thin ice, whose corpuscles are
> minnows, whose drink, sand   .

his ultimate triumph, as the closing sequence by the beach makes clear, is his affirmation of the timeless world of the present—"a

29. See 205:15–19, 236:19–21.

present, a 'present'/ world . . . a snake with its tail in/ its mouth"
(249:8–16):

What's that?
—a duck, a hell-diver? A swimming dog? . . .

When he came out, lifting his knees
through the waves she went to him frisking
her rump awkwardly   .
Wiping his face with his hand he turned
to look back to the waves, then
knocking at his ears, walked up
to stretch out flat on his back in
the hot sand   .   there were some
girls, far down the beach, playing ball.

—must have slept. Got up again, rubbed
the dry sand off and walking a
few steps got into a pair of faded
overalls, slid his shirt on overhand (the
sleeves were still rolled up) shoes,
hat where she had been watching them under
the bank and turned again
to the water's steady roar, as of a distant
waterfall   .   Climbing the
bank, after a few tries, he picked
some beach plums from a low bush and
sampled one of them, spitting the seed out,
then headed inland, followed by the dog.

"I had to think hard," Williams writes in the news release for New Directions,[30] "as to how I was going to end the poem. It wouldn't do to have a grand and soul satisfying conclusion because I didn't

30. See "News from New Directions," May 31, 1951.

see any in my subject. It didn't belong to the subject. It would have been easy to make a great smash up with a 'beautiful' sunset at sea, or a flight of pigeons, love's end and the welter of man's fate. Instead, after the little girl gets herself mixed up at last in the pathetic sophisticate of the great city, no less defeated and understandable, even lovable, than she is herself, we come to the sea at last. Odysseus swims in as man must always do, he doesn't drown, he is too able but, accompanied by his dog, strikes inland again (toward Camden) to begin again."

Index

Amos, 123

Bate, W. J., 153 n.
Blake, William, 10, 19, 20, 80–81, 104 n., 118; *The Marriage of Heaven and Hell*, 10; *The Mental Traveller*, 63 n.; *Milton*, 23–24
Bloom, Harold, 153 n.
Breton, Nicholas, *Phillida and Coridon*, 187 n.
Brinnin, John Malcolm, 12
Browning, Elizabeth Barrett, *Sonnets from the Portuguese*, 51–52

Chaucer, Geoffrey, *The Canterbury Tales*, 178
Coleridge, Samuel Taylor, 41
Crane, Hart, 31 n., 191

Deuteronomy, 27

Eisenstein, Sergei, 73–74
Eliot, T. S., 14, 16, 24, 40–41, 98, 105, 110, 120, 175, 178, 179, 180–81 n., 185, 191; *Ash-Wednesday*, 110; *Four Quartets*, 16, 24; *The Love Song of J. Alfred Prufrock*, 68–70; *The Waste Land*, 36 n., 54, 56, 62, 64, 67, 85–86, 95 ff., 101, 110, 178, 179
Empson, William, 185

Frazer, Sir James George, *The Golden Bough*, 73, 96–97
Frye, Northrop, 111 n.

Ginsberg, Alan, 194–95, 209–11
Graves, Robert, 111
Gray, Thomas, 174

Imagists, 14, 24

Jarrell, Randall, 11, 13, 33
Johnson, Samuel, 144
Joyce, James, 24, 92 n.; *Finnegans Wake*, 92–93 n.; *Stephen Hero*, 24

Keats, John, 112 n., 153 n.; *Ode to Psyche,* 112 n.
Kermode, Frank, 186 n., 187 n.
Koch, Vivienne, 19 n., 30 n., 38 n., 115 n.

Lawrence, D. H., 7, 9, 10, 24; *Swan,* 24
Lewis, R. W. B., 174 n.

Martz, Louis L., 2 n., 11 n., 13, 21–22 n., 58, 62, 63, 160 n.
Matthew, 91

Pater, Walter, *Studies in the History of the Renaissance,* 24
Pearce, Roy Harvey, 12, 55, 63 n., 168
Pound, Ezra, 14, 16, 24, 40–41, 48, 54, 66, 88, 98, 105, 110, 120, 154 n., 171–74, 175, 178, 185, 200 n., 204; *The Cantos,* 62, 118; *A Few Don'ts by an Imagist,* 24; *Hugh Selwyn Mauberley,* 137

Quinn, Sister M. Bernetta, 14, 94–95, 101, 114, 187

Romanticism, 48, 107, 153 n., 211

Santayana, *The Last Puritan,* 133
Shelley, Percy Bysshe, 118, 179; *A Defence of Poetry,* 118, 121 n.; *To Night,* 107 n.
Spears, Monroe K., 159
Stevens, Wallace, 38; *Credences of Summer,* 112 n.; *Esthétique du Mal,* 9; *The Idea of Order at Key West,* 55, 62; *The Man on the Dump,* 42 n.; *Mrs. Alfred Uruguay,* 102 n.; *The Necessary Angel,* 46, 127, 169 n.; *Of Modern Poetry,* 42; *Sunday Morning,* 21

Tennyson, Alfred, 170
Theocritus, 184
Thirlwall, John C., 46 n., 65 n., 141 n., 146, 194 n., 198 n., 204 n.
Tyler, Parker, 92–93 n.

Wagner, Linda Welshimer, 5 n., 19 n.
Whitman, Walt, 54, 62, 131; *Out of the Cradle, Endlessly Rocking,* 211
Williams, William Carlos (works other than *Paterson*)
  Collected Earlier Poems: Danse Russe, 170; *The Flower,* 145; *January Morning,* xiv; *The Locust Tree in Flower,* 125; *Paterson: Episode 17,* 159 n.; *Portrait of a Lady,* 21 n.; *The Red Wheelbarrow,* 6, 125; *Smell!,* 16; *St. Francis Einstein of the Daffodils,* 137; *The Strike* (from *The Wanderer*), 47
  Collected Later Poems: Paterson: the Falls, 26; *The Thoughtful Lover,* xiv

Pictures from Brueghel: Asphodel, That Greeny Flower, xiv, 1, 28, 103–04, 104 n.; *Deep Religious Faith,* 61 n.; *The Descent,* 102; *The Mental Hospital Garden,* 81 n.; *Shadows,* 25

In the American Grain, 1–11, 22, 26, 28 n., 51, 65–67, 86, 87, 89–90, 128–29, 137–39, 149 n., 155, 166, 167, 172–74, 176–77, 211

Autobiography, 62, 172, 181, 182 n.

Selected Essays: "Against the Weather: A Study of the Artist," 153 n.

Selected Letters: to Babette Deutsch (*7/28/47*), 193; to Horace Gregory (*7/22/39*), 139; to Robert Lowell (*1951*), 185; to Marianne Moore (*6/19/51*), 185, 201; to Marianne Moore (*6/23/51*), 184, 187 n., 190; to Parker Tyler (*2/9/46*), 199; to José García Villa (*1950*), 206; to Henry Well (*4/12/50*), 6 n., 109 n.

Miscellaneous: *I Wanted To Write a Poem,* 103 n., 139 n., 152 n., 157 n., 194 n.; *Kora in Hell: Improvisations,* 157 n., 194 n.; *Spring and All,* 25; "The Fatal Blunder," 5 n.; "Letter to an Australian Editor," 48; "Preface," 25; "About the Poem *Paterson*" (in *News from New Directions,* *5/31/51*), 21–22, 50 n., 181 n., 212–13; Speech before English Institute (*1948*), 55; Unpublished letter to James Laughlin (*1/20/39*), 5 n.

Wordsworth, William, 120; *The Prelude,* 23 n.; *Tintern Abbey,* 55

Yeats, W. B., 24, 191; *Chosen,* 24; *Crazy Jane Talks with the Bishop,* 159